VOTING DELIBERATIVELY

RHETORIC AND DEMOCRATIC DELIBERATION
VOLUME 12

Edited by Cheryl Glenn and J. Michael Hogan
The Pennsylvania State University

EDITORIAL BOARD:

Robert Asen (*University of Wisconsin–Madison*)
Debra Hawhee (*The Pennsylvania State University*)
Peter Levine (*Tufts University*)
Steven J. Mailloux (*University of California–Irvine*)
Krista Ratcliffe (*Marquette University*)
Karen Tracy (*University of Colorado–Boulder*)
Kirt Wilson (*The Pennsylvania State University*)
David Zarefsky (*Northwestern University*)

Rhetoric and Democratic Deliberation is a series of groundbreaking monographs and edited volumes focusing on the character and quality of public discourse in politics and culture. It is sponsored by the Center for Democratic Deliberation, an interdisciplinary center for research, teaching, and outreach on issues of rhetoric, civic engagement, and public deliberation.

A complete list of books in this series is located at the back of this volume.

VOTING DELIBERATIVELY

FDR AND THE 1936 PRESIDENTIAL CAMPAIGN

MARY E. STUCKEY

The Pennsylvania State University Press University Park, Pennsylvania

Library of Congress Cataloging-in-Publication Data

Stuckey, Mary E., author.
Voting deliberatively : FDR and the 1936 presidential campaign / Mary E. Stuckey.
    pages   cm — (Rhetoric and democratic deliberation)
Summary: "An analysis of the constituent elements of Franklin Roosevelt's 1936 presidential election campaign, all of which contributed to his victory then and have proved foundational for the way campaigns and politics more broadly are conducted now"—Provided by publisher.
Includes bibliographical references and index.
ISBN 978-0-271-06647-9 (cloth : alk. paper)
ISBN 978-0-271-06648-6 (pbk. : alk. paper)
1. Presidents—United States—Election—1936.
2. Roosevelt, Franklin D. (Franklin Delano), 1882–1945.
3. Deliberative democracy—United States.
I. Title. II. Series: Rhetoric and democratic deliberation.

JK5261936 .S88 2015
324.973'0917—dc23
2014045082

Copyright © 2015 The Pennsylvania State University
All rights reserved
Printed in the United States of America
Published by The Pennsylvania State University Press,
University Park, PA 16802-1003

The Pennsylvania State University Press is a member of the Association of American University Presses.

It is the policy of The Pennsylvania State University Press to use acid-free paper. Publications on uncoated stock satisfy the minimum requirements of American National Standard for Information Sciences—Permanence of Paper for Printed Library Material, ANSI Z39.48–1992.

CONTENTS

Acknowledgments vii

Introduction: Roosevelt and the 1936 Election *1*
1 Creating Public Opinion, Muting the Public's Voice *23*
2 Empowering the Public, Privileging the Candidate *43*
3 Mobilizing the Vote, Containing the Public *66*
4 Speaking for the Public, Empowering the Presidency *89*
   Conclusion: The Mass Public and the Presidency *112*

Notes 123
Bibliography 143
Index 151

ACKNOWLEDGMENTS

Archives are dangerous places, and scholars enter them at our own risk. It is perfectly possible to go into an archive with a limited and clearly defined project in mind, and then become totally ensnared by all the narratives that await the telling and walk out with several more projects that absolutely must be done. I know this because it happened to me, and this book is one of the results.

So my first thanks go to the amazing people at the Franklin D. Roosevelt Presidential Library. They make me—and every researcher—feel extraordinarily welcome, and they are among the most helpful and generous archivists I've ever worked with. I'm especially grateful to Library Director Lynn Bassanese and Assistant Director and Supervisory Archivist Robert Clark. I'm also completely grateful to the various archivists who dug up files for me and were especially patient with my obsession with Emil Hurja: Kirsten Carter, Matthew Hanson, Virginia Lewick, and Sarah Malcolm. Thanks also to Clifford Laube and Jeffrey Urbin.

I also spent some time in Washington, D.C., at the National Archives and the Library of Congress. While there, I was a visiting scholar at the APSA Centennial Center for Political Science and Public Policy and a Presidency Research Group fellow. I'm grateful to APSA for its support. That opportunity also allowed me access to the library at George Washington University, and the librarians there were both friendly and helpful. I very much appreciated the kindness and scholarly acumen of the archivists at the Library of Congress and the National Archives.

I'm also grateful to the wonderful people at Pennsylvania State University Press. Michael Hogan is a wonderful series editor; Kendra Boileau made the process easy and painless. Heartfelt thanks also go to the anonymous reviewers for their help in making the book better. I'm also grateful to Susan Silver, Brian Beer, and the rest of the staff at the Press.

I also need to thank those who have visited the archives with me and who have been kind enough to share my enthusiasm for all things Roosevelt: Linda and Chuck McCarty, Beth Gylys, Jennifer Beese, David Cheshier, Nate Atkinson, Tonia Edwards, Rasha Ramzy, my brother Steve, and my family in general have all been more than tolerant. I'm grateful to have the best group of advisees ever: Steven Stuglin, Stephen Heidt, Reynolds Patterson, Phil Koskta, Zoe Hess Carney, Sara Baugh, Milene Ortega, and John Rountree. You inspire me and make me very proud.

Breaks are as important as the opportunity to do focused work, and I was able to get some magnificent opportunities for time off. So my thanks to Nancy Kassop for the dinners and the geekitude; Pamela and Tim Thompson and also Laura and Jim Parsons, Maren Richter, and Molly McCabe for a couple of the best vacations ever. Thanks also to Brandon and Rachel Inabinet, who almost convinced me that South Carolina is not the scariest place on the planet.

Speaking of the opportunity to do focused work, I could not have completed this book in such a timely manner without the support of Georgia State University's Research Services Administration. I was fortunate enough to receive both a Scholarly Support Grant, which enabled me to get a head start on the research on this book while finishing another, and a Time and Travel Grant, which allowed me to finish the research. The final draft of the book was finished while I was on a leave provided by the College of Arts and Sciences at GSU. I am immensely grateful for the support. I presented a first take of the project as "Inventing Presidential Elections: FDR and the 1936 Campaign" at the annual meeting of the American Political Science Association in 2013.

I am especially grateful to my mother, to whom this book is dedicated. She taught me that the things we can never fully achieve are also the ones most worth striving for, and she provides an example of a life well lived and well worth emulating. I love you, Mom.

INTRODUCTION:
ROOSEVELT AND THE 1936 ELECTION

A few short months before the election, the outcome seemed anything but certain. Both internal White House polls and the public polls conducted by the media supported the wide range of available anecdotal evidence: the president was in trouble. His first election, in the wake of a thoroughly discredited Republican administration, had once seemed to hold the promise of Democratic dominance for the foreseeable future. But continuing economic problems, a controversial domestic agenda, and a foreign policy that seemed weak and vacillating eroded the administration's support among the mass public. The administration was attacked every day on the nation's mass media and the president faced vicious and unrelenting criticism from both the Right and the Left, some of it aimed at his policies, much of it directed at the person of the president himself. Such criticism even escalated into the formation of a new political party dedicated, it appeared, exclusively to undermining the president and attacking his programs. From all the available evidence, then, it seemed unlikely that the president was about to make history.

But his reelection was indeed historic. Franklin Delano Roosevelt won the 1936 election with nearly 61 percent of the vote, capturing forty-six of the forty-eight states, losing only in Maine and Vermont. Looking back at that result and knowing, as we do now, the entirety of the legacy left to us by FDR, it is easy to forget how contestable—and how contested—his administration actually was.[1] It is also easy to overlook the innovations of that campaign and the consequences they had for the practices of American democracy.[2] This book examines that campaign with an eye toward understanding an underexamined moment in our national history and analyzing how the elements of that campaign reveal contemporary patterns in American elections as deliberative events.[3] Specifically, I argue that there are several constituent elements of Roosevelt's 1936 election campaign, none of which have received appropriate attention, and all of which contributed to his victory then and have proved foundational for the way campaigns and politics more broadly are conducted now. Each of these elements affects the ways in which the American mass public participates in and is understood through national elections. They are also integral to contemporary patterns of democratic deliberation. Roosevelt's conduct of the 1936 election is a particularly good way to access these elements because it stands at the intersection of differing understandings of campaigning and American politics. That election thus allows us to look both backward and forward, to more fully comprehend what has been gained and was has been lost as the center of American politics shifted from states to the federal level and American influence began to be felt internationally.

I am not positing this election as the moment of breakdown in the American system, in which all prior elections were characterized by healthy forms of deliberation and all later ones evidence of the collapse of deliberation and democracy. The problems of democratic deliberation in a republic are legion and have never been solved. There has been no golden age of American democracy in which an inclusive polity has carefully debated relevant policy and in which republican forms of representation have been perfectly enacted. In fact, there is and always has been a tension between inclusion and efficiency, and there has always been a tendency among those who are included to generalize their interests to that of the "public interest."[4] This election is interesting partly because those problems and potential solutions were very much on the minds of those involved in the Roosevelt campaign. Their solutions, such as they were, had some beneficial and also some perverse effects, both of which are with us today. It is with the hope of better understanding their politics as well as our own that I focus on 1936.

I look closely at four elements of the Roosevelt campaign as revealing of the shifts in the way the public and its deliberative role in American politics are understood. I treat "the public" here in the informal, rather than in the Habermasian sense. That is, I am not interested in how these practices created or failed to create a healthy theoretical public sphere so much as I am concerned with how practical politicians sought to include, exclude, organize, mobilize, and manage the electorate. As Janet M. Atwill has noted, models of civic virtue are tied to political practice.[5] By closely examining those practices, we can learn a great deal about how citizenship was understood then and continues to inform our contemporary politics.

Each of the elements I examine involves something of a paradox of deliberation and democracy in the American republic. First, the 1936 Roosevelt campaign involved both older and emerging models of assessing public opinion. That campaign made extensive use of personal and partisan contacts and also developed new methods of aggregating and tracking opinion by polling. This meant that FDR and his aides had a broad and deep understanding of the electorate as a public and could carefully calibrate how they understood its opinions. As Roosevelt sought to include a greater number of (white) people in the public and to open up American politics and expand his coalition, it became concomitantly more difficult to apprehend either the public itself or its collective views. Public-opinion polling allowed Roosevelt to aggregate opinion but would increasingly do so at the expense of other, more nuanced ways of understanding that opinion. The public, then, became larger and less well understood, more able to participate in politics and also less able to articulate its preferences.

Second, the 1936 Roosevelt campaign, relying as it did on the mobilization of a broad swath of the mass public, was one of the first national campaigns to depend on what we now call the "ground game." Scholars and pundits alike consider Franklin D. Roosevelt an eloquent speaker, a master of radio, a public communicator par excellence and understand these traits as fundamental to his political success.[6] Focusing on Roosevelt's communicative skill, however, can lead us to overlook his dedication to organizational politics.[7] His 1936 campaign used a variety of mobilization techniques that are now commonplace but which were, for their time, revolutionary. As politics based on elites increasingly gave way to mass politics, mobilization of a diverse electorate became a critical component of national politics, and the president, rather than the party, became the center of political organization. Roosevelt worked with his party, but also relied on extrapartisan organizations. The paradox here is that as the nation became in some ways more democratic, it did so within structures that were specifically republican, putting major stresses on the system. The federal government's response to those stresses led to an increase in national and presidential power, which undermined both the democratic and republican impulses of national institutions and weakened the ability of the public to articulate itself through its political institutions. Roosevelt helped give us candidate-centered campaigns and president-centered government.

Third, faced with the need to mobilize the mass public, Roosevelt in 1936 approached the polity as a composite of different kinds of interests. Paradoxically, then, he created a unified coalition by first fragmenting the electorate into groups, some of which had significantly more access than others. Mobilizing the public by demographic group created a certain view of public opinion, enabling the development of interest-group politics and a group-based, pluralistic view of what and who the public are.[8] Voters and citizens were less able, as individuals, to articulate interests that concerned government. Instead, individuals came to be understood as constituted by their group membership, identities that either facilitated access or precluded it. As the electorate expanded (and it remained restricted in important ways during the Roosevelt years), national campaigns engaged in increasingly mediated ways of segmenting the public into fragmented units that could be identified and mobilized on the basis of specific attributes—either ascriptive (women), economic (blue-collar workers), or demographic (Protestants). But this practice also fractured political identities in ways that may not be productive for the practices of republican citizenship. As Ira Katznelson recently noted, with politics organized around interest groups, procedural democracy came to dominate the "common good" as a structuring element of the national state.[9] Group membership was specifically connected with self-interest and the conception of citizenship narrowed.

Finally, I examine the ways in which FDR himself sought to reconcile these paradoxes through his public rhetoric. That rhetoric depended, in large part, on the creation of a new kind of political authority, grounded in the person of the president. While serving to nationalize American politics and helping to create an American state, Roosevelt's rhetoric also forged a personality-centered view of national politics that tends to reduce deliberative possibilities, impoverishing discussion of issues, institutions, and processes and focusing instead on the character of candidates and elected officials. The 1930s were notable for the rise of plebiscitary politics, which are associated with a personalized understanding of politics, reliance on public opinion, and the spectacular: government had increasingly to be seen to be understood as legitimate.[10] Roosevelt enabled the rhetorical presidency and the consequent imbalance in presidential power vis-à-vis that of Congress.[11] Paradoxically, then, FDR sought to facilitate deliberative politics, often stressing the need for an educated and active electorate, and at the same time engaged in political practices that disabled some of the deliberative potential of national elections.

In the short run, these practices contributed to both a winning campaign in 1936 and a coalition that dominated American politics for decades. Equally important, in my view, is that they continue to affect the ways in which the public and its opinions are understood by those in power. They also affect the ways in which the public deliberates during elections and the kinds of questions that are the subject of their deliberation. Roosevelt probably never intended any of these consequences. But they are unmistakably rooted in his conception of politics and political leadership. The contours of that leadership were made abundantly clear during his first term and especially in the kinds of support and opposition generated during that term that formed the basis for his coalition building during the 1936 election.

Prologue to the First Term

October 29, 1929, "Black Tuesday," is the conventional marker of the beginning of the Great Depression and the primary cause of Roosevelt's first election in November 1932. Between the crash and the election stood three years of deepening economic crisis. Attempting to protect the nation's farmers, Congress passed the Smoot-Hawley Act in 1930, which led to an eruption of retaliatory measures in Europe and drastically disrupted international trade. On December 11, 1930, the Bank of the United States failed, creating a symbolic as well as a material crisis. Within six months European nations declared a moratorium on repayments of their war debts, further disrupting the American economy and the international markets on which it increasingly depended. By 1933 the official unemployment rate was 25 percent. Unofficial sources put it much higher.[12] Cities were becoming more dangerous; the homeless seemed ever more threatening and violence ever more possible.[13]

The growing world economic crisis was compounded by a series of international political crises. Japan invaded Manchuria and the government of Germany, long insecure, surrendered to the democratically elected National Socialist Party under the leadership of Adolf Hitler. In the face of these events, Americans, mindful of the cost of World War I and uncertain of its benefits, remained firmly isolationist. They had, it seemed, more than enough trouble at home without seeking it elsewhere in the world.

Their domestic trouble only got worse. In the United States insecurity deepened into panic as state banks failed. By March 4, 1933, these banks had closed in thirty-four of the forty-eight states. Between 1929 and 1933 the Gross National

Product had fallen by 30 percent and industrial production fell by 60 percent.[14] The nation's citizens had no safety net. Hundreds of thousands of Americans lost their jobs, their livelihoods, and their homes. Herbert Hoover's response, deemed insufficient when it wasn't considered overtly hostile to the suffering, contributed to his defeat and the first election of Franklin Roosevelt.[15] FDR's mandate was to do something—maybe even anything—to end the financial crisis. His administration, it was clear, would be judged on its ability to restore the national economy and the nation's confidence. The first task would prove considerably harder than the second.

The Hundred Days

Upon entering office, Roosevelt certainly made good on his promise of "undelayed action" at the behest of an empowered chief executive.[16] Between his inauguration on March 4 and the final day of the legislative session on June 16, 1933, Congress passed and the president signed a bewildering array of legislation. One analyst notes, "The Hundred Days was more than the greatest burst of legislation in American history—it was a revolution."[17] Major initiatives included the Emergency Banking Relief Act, the Economy Act, the Beer-Wine Revenue Act, the Agricultural Adjustment Act, the Federal Securities Act, and the Banking Act. Congress also authorized the Farm Credit Administration, the Civilian Conservation Corps, the Tennessee Valley Authority, and the Federal Emergency Relief Administration. The United States was taken off the gold standard and its workers were given a thirty-hour workweek. Homeowners were allowed to refinance their homes and avoid foreclosure. Farmers were provided with subsidies. Roosevelt gave the first of his fireside chats. The nation, stultified by the effects of the Depression, was now invigorated by the sense of movement and activity emanating from Washington.

The National Industrial Recovery Act was the most important New Deal program. It was signed into law on June 16, 1933, the last legislation of the Hundred Days. The cornerstone of the New Deal, it was "more than a government program. It was equal parts spiritual revival, political campaign, and wartime mobilization."[18] Administered through the National Recovery Administration (NRA), the act was troubled in many ways and is usually considered a programmatic failure.[19] It nonetheless established the groundwork for many domestic reforms, including worker safety standards, more humane working conditions, and collective bargaining. The NRA's famous blue eagle, patterned on an American Indian motif, became the logo for the Philadelphia Eagles football franchise, one indication of how deeply New Deal programs permeated the national culture.[20]

By the end of the Hundred Days, Roosevelt accrued more direct administrative authority than any president in history.[21] He gained enormous control over the economy, foreign trade, gold prices, and the domestic conduct of business. He put thousands of young men to work for the Civilian Conservation Corps.[22] By the end of its run, individuals funded by Federal Emergency Relief Administration alone "taught over one and half million adults to read and write, ran nursery schools for children from low-income families, and helped one hundred thousand students to attend college."[23] The government had never before employed so many people doing so many diverse projects. Roosevelt established himself as the undisputed head of a burgeoning national government. The New Deal wasn't just a Democratic program or a federal program; it was Roosevelt's program. While the nation had seen strong presidents and even occasional strong partisan legislative programs before, under FDR the party in power and its policies were dominated by the single iconic image of the president himself.[24] Not since Andrew Jackson's war on the bank had a legislative program been so strongly associated with an individual president.[25] Roosevelt encouraged this identification, as Jackson had before him, but he also coupled it with an institutional apparatus that answered to the chief executive, changing the ways in which Americans and their government thought about and acted toward the president.[26] This trajectory was clear in the Hundred Days; it extended over the entire first term.

Support and Opposition

While the Hundred Days remain one of the single most impressive legislative achievements of the modern presidency and are still the (unreasonable) bar by which other new presidencies are measured, the New Deal is not reducible to those achievements. Other important developments occurred in the first term. Not only did FDR begin the processes of altering the structures of the federal government and the role of the political parties in elections and governance, but he continued to sponsor significant legislation as well. Although always criticized on the one hand for not doing enough and while it was always clear to the Left that he was more of a reformer than a radical, he advocated programs that were, for the time, remarkable innovations. Three other programs under the Second New Deal deserve special mention under this heading. First, the Rural Electrification Administration brought electricity to rural parts of the country, forever changing the way rural Americans lived. Second, the Wagner Labor Relations Act guaranteed workers the right to unionize. These two pieces of legislation, like Social Security, passed in 1935, depended on federal administration, and, at the same time, reached deeply into both the American heartland and cities, forging changes that altered the face of national politics. Roosevelt fought hard for all these programs and saw them as critical to his political legacy. Conservative resistance threatened both his power and his legacy, a fact that was clear to everyone on May 27, 1935, Black Monday.

On that day, the United States Supreme Court definitively declared many elements of the New Deal unconstitutional. In a unanimous decision in the *Schechter* case, the "nine old men" on the Court presented Roosevelt with his single biggest political defeat to date and demonstrated, as nothing else had, the president's political vulnerability.[27] In response to the Court's decision, Roosevelt held one of his most impressive press conferences. Speaking at length and without notes, he discoursed on the Constitution, the Court, and the role of both in American political life. He made a clear case for executive supremacy in the face of the Court's recalcitrance, but the Court had the last word; the National Industrial Recovery Act was dead.[28] New Deal reforms may have "saved democracy in eight days," but it was by no means clear either that they were to be proven effective or that they were consistent with the Constitution. The first question is still debated.[29] The second would, in later years, cause the loudest uproar of Roosevelt's long and tumultuous presidency.

In the short term, the voices objecting to the New Deal and to FDR's leadership came from both the Right and the Left. The range of this criticism both threatened his reelection by potentially splitting the vote and eventually assisted it by making his claims to be centrist more reasonable. In the long term, as the political practices associated with the New Deal became integral to the wider practices of American politics, these criticisms also had significant staying power, lasting not only through the Roosevelt administration but also well beyond.

ATTACKS FROM THE RIGHT

One of the most persistent criticisms of FDR was that he aspired to or exercised dictatorial power. Unfounded as this criticism now appears, it was much more credible at the time, as Roosevelt increased the power of the presidency in profoundly personal ways.³⁰ He was variously accused of communistic, socialistic, and fascist leanings, accusations that sometimes served as general expressions of fear of this president, presidential power in general, and specific New Deal policies. But it was not only about labels and generalized fears. Serious people made serous arguments about the dangers of increased federal and presidential power and about the consequences of particular programs. The NRA, for instance, caused consternation among business people, and the nation in general was outraged by the Agricultural Adjustment Act's destruction of crops and the killing of livestock.³¹

It seemed to some that the president was trying to control everything. In January 1934, for example, he canceled all domestic air-mail contracts, potentially crippling the young aviation industry, and assigned the Army Air Corps to mail delivery. The airmen lacked the experience, the training, and the technology required for the job, and ten men died. The industry and the public were outraged. It seemed clear that the national government could not, in fact, outperform industry.³² The air-mail debacle represented the first moment in which the charges of despotism and even communism began to gain real traction.³³

In August 1934 Jouett Shouse and conservative Democrats in combination with some Republicans formed the American Liberty League, whose mission was to "defend and uphold the Constitution," protect property rights, and "combat radical trends."³⁴ Other well-known Democrats joined the league, most prominently former Roosevelt ally and previous Democratic standard-bearer, Al Smith.³⁵ Despite the passion of those who joined, the league was never a very successful endeavor. It was both small (estimates were that even by late 1935, it had only seventy-five thousand members) and ineffective.³⁶ Partly, the problem was that the league was unable to recruit moderates in any significant numbers and soon became the haven of the vehement opposition to Roosevelt and everything he stood for on the one hand and of those who seemed more dedicated to their own financial interest than the good of the country on the other. Arthur Krock, for example, wrote that the league seemed to be "created for the sole purpose of bringing back the Old Deal and its evils, including the placement of private property over everything else."³⁷

Members of the league and their allies had never supported the president, and their opposition meant little. More important was the disaffection of former allies. Father Charles E. Coughlin, widely known as the "radio priest," was one of the most vocal opponents of the administration and claimed millions in his audience.³⁸ Once a strong advocate of the New Deal, he became disaffected and began to use his massive popularity to attack rather than support the administration and its actions. Coughlin's opposition led to the formation of a third party in 1936 (the Union Party), which served as a vehicle for his increasingly rabid anti-Semitism and his opposition to Roosevelt and the New Deal.

Other Roosevelt opponents were more easily disregarded, although their arguments, in the hands of less flawed interlocutors, continued to pose problems for the administration. Former president Hoover put his sour grapes on display, never missing an opportunity to refer to the "socialism" of the Democrats in general and FDR in particular. He claimed that they "wore the color of despotism . . . the color of Fascism . . . the color of Socialism."[39] Such personalized attacks against Roosevelt were readily dismissed.[40] The backlash caused by such accusations redounded to the president's favor as the very shrillness of Roosevelt's enemies worked against them.[41]

More worrying than the personalized and easily dismissed fulminations of politicians like Hoover was the constant criticism from newspaper owners and publishers. Roosevelt commanded enormous affection from the reporters who covered his administration.[42] The same could not be said for those who employed those reporters. Chief among his critics in the press stood William Randolph Hearst, who told his reporters to refer to the president's program as the "Raw Deal" rather than the New Deal and who opposed the president in every way he could in all his papers.[43] So great was his influence that in 1936 it became a campaign issue.[44]

Business people, once grateful to Roosevelt, and then increasingly suspicious of him, were convinced by 1935 that he was perpetrating class warfare.[45] Roosevelt's tax policies made business apoplectic.[46] They worried about the rising cost of government, they worried about the centralization of power, and they worried about the increases in regulation critical to many New Deal programs. They had supported FDR, early in his administration, fearful that without drastic action, the economy would collapse. Once a measure of stability returned, however, they resisted further federal action as likely to cripple private enterprise and destroy individual initiative.

So throughout the first term, opposition to FDR and the New Deal built on the Right. This opposition was not unified but ranged from the frenzied ranting of Father Coughlin to the more moderate complaints of many business people. This range was extensive enough to make it difficult for them to find a single candidate or a clear program to offer in place of Roosevelt. They agreed only on the need to replace him. Their best hope, it appeared throughout 1935, might be for the Left itself to fracture and dismantle the New Deal and the administration from within the Democratic Party.

ATTACKS FROM THE LEFT

Given the continuing economic dislocations, it is hardly surprising that Roosevelt, once hailed as the nation's savior, would come under increasingly heavy criticism as salvation remained elusive. Nor is it surprising that other politicians on the Left would begin to claim that recovery was more likely under their policies and their leadership. By far, the most dangerous of these politicians was Huey P. Long, once governor, by 1930 a U.S. senator from Louisiana; the Kingfish, larger than life, bombastic, improbable, and immeasurably wily.[47] Originally a strong Roosevelt supporter, Long eventually broke with the administration and came to represent, more than any other individual, the growing tide of dissent from the Left.[48] He appeared both ready and willing to challenge the president in 1936 but was assassinated before any such bid could be realized. His successor, Gerald K. Smith, presided over the death of Long's Share the Wealth movement rather than its success, but the disaffection with Roosevelt in many quarters remained, and it appeared possible that it could be mobilized if the right standard-bearer could be found.

Long's movement remained largely restricted to the South, but similar challenges appeared in other regions as well. Politicians like Upton Sinclair of California and the LaFollettes of Wisconsin were cause for concern lest they peel off enough support in crucial states to cost Roosevelt the election. More threatening was Dr. Francis Townsend, who had a national following. Townsend proposed a naive and unworkable plan of supplying every elderly American a guaranteed income on the conditions that they promised to stop working (thus opening up jobs for younger people) and spend it (thus priming the economy). The simplicity of the plan was appealing, at least among those most likely to benefit.

These various movements and figures made it increasingly evident that the "forgotten man," as FDR had famously characterized suffering citizens during the 1932 campaign, was not necessarily going to offer Roosevelt unqualified support in the 1936 election. They indicated potential trouble in almost every region and with almost every demographic. Indeed, the common thread, if there was one, uniting the adherents of Long, Coughlin, and Townsend, was the fact that they were among the nation's most vulnerable: they were, variously, rural and elderly, unwilling to abide by the New Deal's progressive stance on modernization and worried about the direction toward which the nation seemed to be inexorably headed.[49]

Problems for FDR extended beyond the dissatisfaction of these citizens as well. Roosevelt also encountered major problems from organized labor. In January 1934 a longshoreman's strike shut down the ports in San Francisco; strikers shut down mills on the eastern seaboard and into South Carolina. Strikes also hit the Midwest. Apparently no region, no industry was invulnerable to increasingly militant American workers. While 324,210 workers had been involved in strikes in 1932, a year later that number had risen to 1.6 million. The strikes were also increasingly violent, approaching levels not seen since 1919.[50] Those without jobs were also increasingly angry. After two full years of New Deal programs and Rooseveltian promises, one-fifth of the workforce remained unemployed.[51] A class war seemed actually possible.[52] Such fears contributed to the precipitous drop in the president's popularity.[53] Between the unrelenting attacks from the Right and the various alternatives to his administration being offered on the Left, things looked bleak for the president as 1934 edged into 1935. But he also had considerable sources of support and a deep reservoir of political skill.

SUPPORTING FDR

Roosevelt's program had been overwhelmingly endorsed in the 1934 midterm elections, after which the Democratic ascendency in Congress seemed assured.[54] Those elections were also a bit ominous in that they indicated not only Roosevelt's popularity but also the nation's willingness to move to the Left.[55] Roosevelt himself, however, was only willing to go so far and no farther. Despite the charges constantly leveled against him, he was neither an aspiring communist nor a dictator. Roosevelt always insisted—correctly—that the New Deal was more about recovery and reform than revolution. His first priority was relief. The government under FDR took on new responsibilities for the care and succor of its neediest citizens. His second priority was recovery, and his third, reform. He wanted to alter the relationship between the national political system and the national economy so that the former could exercise more control over the latter. In this, he stopped far short of proffering socialism under a democratic guise. In offering relief and reform, he also sought to protect both capitalism and democracy. But he argued that for either capitalism or democracy to survive, they needed to be dominated by a chief executive who sat astride a truly national government. And more than anything else, the national debate during these years centered in the questions of the proper role of government and the proper role of the president within that government. Thus, Roosevelt put himself at the center of the 1936 election.

Given the problems with and the eventual invalidation of the National Industrial Recovery Act, by 1935 FDR put tremendous emphasis on Social Security as his signature program. Roosevelt insisted that the program had to be self-funding, a fact that became, as the president foresaw it would, its greatest strength and biggest weakness.[56] This requirement limited the number of people who could be covered and deepened the inequities that already operated against people of color, women, and the very poor.[57] But it also helped ensure its passage in the short term and protected the program over the long term. It became difficult if not impossible for anyone to challenge the system, much less to consider eliminating it. The program made a tremendous difference to those who were most vulnerable during the Depression, helping keep food on the table, heat in the house, and the wolf from the door. Significant numbers of Social Security recipients became or remained Roosevelt voters.

He also had the support of many mainstream Democrats who feared the return of what Krock called the "Old Deal" and who worried about the possibility of real revolution as economic and social dislocations threatened political ones as well. He had a promising relationship with some Republicans as well. Because of its emphasis on social justice, progressive Republicans were much happier with the Second New Deal than they had been with the first. They were against the more conservative alternatives to FDR, but they remained reluctant supporters of the administration and its president.[58] Mostly, they were confused and left in some political disarray as Democrats seemed to take the mantle of liberal reform from them.[59] They wanted to back many New Deal policies but not the New Deal's president or his party. And they seemed increasingly disconnected from the Republican Party and its leadership.

Going into the 1936 campaign, then, the nation had been long consumed with conversations about the damaged economy and how best to repair it, about the national government and how much power to give it, and about the nation itself and how best to lead it. Roosevelt had a wide-ranging, if not always coherent, set of answers to these questions. His various opponents had a variety of objections to his policies and a broad range of alternatives. The election was, therefore, practically a textbook case of the possibilities for deliberation in a democratic republic. It was a referendum on the president and a test of the relationship he had forged with the American people. It was also a proving ground for his theories of governance—theories that turned on the new cultural emphasis on science and efficiency, manifested in public-opinion polls; that depended on the mobilization of the mass public; that understood the public as composed of economic and ascriptive groups; and that sought to unify those groups through an avowedly nationalistic set of rhetorical appeals. The 1936 election validated both these theories and the president's leadership and proved to be the pivotal moment in the creation of the New Deal coalition and the practice of American elections.

The 1936 Campaign

We think of presidential campaigns as confined processes, engaged in between candidates from two major parties who seek to influence voters in specifically targeted states. They are, however, also more than that. They are national conversations about the policies, parties, and people who will govern the nation, and they involve members of the mass public, organized by party but also along the lines of interest groups and demographics, as well as unaffiliated and sometimes even uninterested citizens. Elections are opportunities to engage in debate as well as to make decisions. The outcomes of elections thus are not reducible to counting votes and determining winners and losers.

By that standard, the 1936 election settled many matters. The Republican Party was unequivocally routed as the election results seemed to disable it for the foreseeable future. The election all but destroyed the American Liberty League, which maintained a nominal and ineffective national office but disbanded all its state offices in the wake of Roosevelt's victory. It also solidified FDR's power, making him all but unassailable until he overreached even the broad parameters allowed him and attempted to pack the Court and purge Congress. And it set in motion specific kinds of political practices that outlasted Roosevelt and all his supporters and opponents. To help understand these outcomes, I offer here a quick overview of the election.

Roosevelt's opponents began to gear up for the election long before the polls actually opened or the campaign officially began. The American Liberty League, for instance, was actively campaigning against the president from its formation in 1934. So active was the league, in fact, that many members of the public began to see it as an organization designed by the wealthy for the express purpose of defeating the president and all his works, causing resentment among New Deal supporters.⁶⁰ Citizens of Tulsa, Oklahoma, for example, passed a series of resolutions condemning the league and its attacks on the New Deal.⁶¹ Others wrote to the president and to the campaign, expressing their fears about but also their support for the league.⁶²

Despite its relative ineffectiveness, the White House saw the potential for the Liberty League to both broaden and organize opposition to the president.⁶³ One appeal was especially worrying: the league consistently argued that Roosevelt was acting against the Constitution, a concern that seemed to be infinitely more plausible than most of its accusations.⁶⁴ On this ground, the league seemed potentially able to arouse voters concerned about the nature and extent of federal and presidential power under the New Deal. Had it stuck to that argument, the league might have enjoyed considerable success.⁶⁵ But it didn't. Instead, league speakers seemed eager to vent their most personal antagonisms and to give voice to the most ridiculous claims. When Al Smith called Roosevelt a communist in January 1936 and threatened to "take a walk" rather than vote Democratic in the coming election, the resulting backlash devastated the league.⁶⁶ The president's popularity skyrocketed.⁶⁷

With friends like the league, Alfred (Alf) Landon's campaign needed no enemies. But enemies and opponents he had, both within and outside the Republican Party. Landon was a fairly moderate Republican with a tendency to support New Deal programs and a good record on civil liberties, having fought the Ku Klux Klan in his home state of Kansas. Essentially, he owed his nomination to the Republican recognition that their best hope for victory depended on reinvigorating the East-West coalition of the past. Without the West, Republicans had virtually no chance.⁶⁸ As Walter Lippmann noted in early 1935, "the gulf which separates men like Norris and Nye and Cutting from fellow Republicans like Hastings and Delaware is deep, and the Republican problem is to bridge it."⁶⁹ With Landon's nomination, that goal seemed to be within reach. His supporters tended to be those who thought FDR was spending too much and becoming too enamored of the dole, thus threatening American values, and was, perhaps, too reliant on a staff of "planners" for the nation's good.⁷⁰ "The apparent strategy of the Republican campaign was to build on the conservative business interests that were anti-Roosevelt; to draw away those agricultural elements in the Midwest that were dissatisfied with the Agricultural Adjustment Act; to win back the Progressive Republicans; to attract some of the labor vote; and to win over all those who were fearful of one or more aspects of the New Deal."⁷¹ This was not a bad strategy, for the disaffection with Roosevelt was real, but it required a persuasive and consistent campaign, and this the Republicans did not deliver—Landon, for instance, didn't make a single campaign speech for some two months after his nomination, leaving the field open to a series of Roosevelt surrogates, all charged with making the case for the New Deal.[72]

Landon's very moderation, which Republicans hoped would bridge the party's factions, actually exacerbated the split in conservative ranks. Some three days after Landon earned the Republican nomination, Huey Long's political heir, Gerald K. Smith, improbably joined to Father Coughlin and Francis Townsend, announced the formation of a new political party dedicated to defeating both Roosevelt and the "communistic philosophy of Frankfurter, Ickes, Hopkins, and Wallace."[73] The Union Party nominated as their candidate North Dakota congressman William Lemke, a former populist. The party threatened to peel off support for Landon, and his silence gave center stage back to the more extreme elements of Roosevelt's opposition, enabling the widespread belief that this opposition was increasingly hysterical. Conservatives certainly didn't seem fit to run a country in continued crisis.

Meanwhile, Roosevelt ran what he called a "non-political" campaign, taking a "drought-inspection tour" of the Midwest and refusing to admit that he was interested in politics at all, busy as he was running the country. Landon's refusal to campaign, fairly common in previous elections, created problems for him in the context of a highly mediated and vocal campaign. Roosevelt, who also refused to campaign formally, made sure that as president he received more than a fair share of national attention, making it clear to the public that he was acting on their behalf and consistently defending the New Deal. Despite his claims that he was not interested in the election, he did take the time to orchestrate the Democratic Convention, where he managed the process of repealing he "two-thirds rule," which minimized the influence of the South and would be vital to his reelection campaign in 1940.[74] Behind the scenes, he began the most intensive polling operation in presidential history, while his chief political aide, Postmaster General Jim Farley, managed a more personal, but no less intensive, survey of Democratic Party leaders. The ground game had also begun, with the efforts of the Good Neighbor League and the Committee of One organizing in preparation for the coming election, and the party's Women's Division, which had been organizing for over a year, gearing up for its final mobilization effort. These activities were entirely invisible as far as the president's public activities were concerned, however. He was dedicated to the pretense that he was running the country, not a campaign.[75]

This serene refusal to engage his opposition provided a sharp contrast to the ever-escalating rhetoric of the conservatives. The moderate and reasonable Landon was largely absent; Coughlin and his allies increasingly absurd. Throughout the summer FDR concentrated on being presidential. So determinedly nonpolitical was he, in fact, that Roosevelt didn't actually acknowledge he was running for reelection until late September, in a speech at Syracuse University. His first announced "campaign trip" began October 1, 1936, a mere month before the actual election.[76]

When he did openly enter the campaign, though, he came out swinging, unleashing a series of speeches in which he took the battle straight to his opponents. He tied the Republican Party to the Liberty League and to the worst excesses of the moneyed class, contrasting their selfishness and greed with the humanistic policies of his administration. He defended his record and challenged that of his opposition, which he characterized as being made up of "economic royalists," who not only opposed his actions in defense of the "forgotten man" but showed base ingratitude for his actions in saving capitalism. And in the campaign's thundering finish, in an almost unbelievably antagonistic speech coming from a sitting president, FDR drew clear lines of demarcation: he said of his opponents that "they had begun to consider the Government of the United States as a mere appendage to their own affairs. We know now that Government by organized money is just as dangerous as Government by organized mob. Never before in all our history have these forces been so united against one candidate as they stand today. They are unanimous in their hate for me—and I welcome their hatred. I should like to have it said of my first Administration that in it the forces of selfishness and of lust for power met their match. I should like to have it said of my second Administration that in it these forces met their master."[77] In making it a class-based campaign, Roosevelt capitalized on the biggest mistake the Republicans could have made. They decided to run a campaign based on attacking Social Security, thus apparently confirming every argument the president made against them.[78]

For the Republicans, Social Security exemplified everything that was wrong and dangerous in the New Deal. It was expensive, it was run by the federal government, it would increase taxes on working people, and it benefited some workers at the expense of others.[79] But these arguments, as reasonable as they were, also made it possible for Democrats to plausibly characterize the Republicans as oblivious to the very real need among suffering Americans. While there was a clear basis in political principle for their arguments, grounded as they were in the belief in limited government and the protection of individual liberty, that liberty also implied governmental inaction in the face of a human crisis. Roosevelt, on the other hand, made the easing of that crisis one of his foundational political principles and made the Republicans the foil of his crusade to save American capitalism and democracy by rendering government sensitive and responsive to its neediest citizens.

Roosevelt's campaign was characterized by a tendency to act fairly conservatively but to talk increasingly divisively. This combination allowed him on the one hand to amplify the stakes of the contest and on the other to protect himself against charges of socialism and communism. He could be understood as protecting the system in general, an appeal important to moderates, and as protecting the common people against the depredations of the powerful. When the Republicans railed against Roosevelt's pandering to the poor and promising them relief in exchange for votes, this fed the perception that they were interested only in protecting their own economic interest. In a September 1936 "Presidential Trial Heat" survey focused on "reliefers," 75.1 percent of those on relief favored Roosevelt over Landon's 17.5 percent. Lemke polled a mere 5.3 percent; Norman Thomas, who might have been expected to do better, trailed with 1.6 percent of the reliefers' vote. By the end of the campaign, these voters were joined by millions of others in favoring FDR.[80]

The 1936 election ratified the New Deal coalition, a collection of urban northern ethnics and northern African Americans, Jews, Catholics, and southern Democrats. That election is the first for which we have national demographic data. Those data indicate that Roosevelt "failed to carry the upper income group, the businessmen, or the professional group, but his popularity was great in the lower income group, the workers—especially those in the trade unions—the farmers, and the unemployed. Among the religious groups he was most popular with Catholics, Jews, and non-Church members, barely capturing the Protestant vote."[81] FDR earned 86 percent of the Jewish vote, 81 percent of Catholics, 80 percent of the labor vote, 76 percent of the southern vote and the same number of African Americans in northern cities.[82] The Republican Party seemed damaged beyond repair. Equally important, the socialist share of the vote dropped from 872,000 in 1932 to a mere 187,572 in 1936, providing clear evidence that FDR had forestalled any challenges from the Left for the foreseeable future.[83] Most impressive was Roosevelt's strength in urban areas: out of the nation's 106 cities with a population of a hundred thousand or more, Roosevelt won 102.[84] The Republicans had outspent the Democrats by more than $3 million, a monstrous sum in those Depression times, and in return had gotten very little.[85] By every measure, Roosevelt's margin of victory was unprecedented. The antagonism that underlay the campaign and the hubris thus created contributed to Roosevelt's two biggest political miscalculations, court packing and the congressional purge. In the long run, however, the changes forged in that election remade the American state and the political processes that allowed it to function.

Previous histories that include discussions of the 1936 election emphasize the elements I have covered here: FDR's vulnerability before the campaign, Landon's weakness as a candidate, the ways in which the stridency of the conservative opposition undercut their case against the president, Roosevelt's astute refusal to enter the fray, and the power and divisive potential of his rhetoric once he did. These histories sometimes mention, but do not emphasize, the other important elements of that campaign that form the basis of this book: the quantity and the quality of the information Roosevelt and his campaign acquired, both through anecdotal and statistical means; the importance of organizations such as the Good Neighbor League and the Committee of One; the mobilization of the vote facilitated by understanding it in terms of interests, exemplified through entities such as the Democratic National Committee's Women's Division; and the ways in which these organizational efforts fused with the rhetorical strategies and practices of this most adept candidate. These elements and their interactions are highlighted in the pages that follow.

The goal here is not to explain the Roosevelt victory, although, clearly, the conduct of the campaign contributed to that victory. But the lessons of the victory are as important as the victory itself, and those included practices that helped candidates and elected officials manage elections and policy making but that also had consequences for the deliberative possibilities among a mass public. The depth and breadth of understanding the nation's attitudes about policy and those who made it that was available to FDR has narrowed to become summary data in public-opinion polls, which reveals useful but very different kinds of information. The 1936 Roosevelt campaign depended on the invention of a ground game and the mobilization of supporters, an innovation that infused local politics with national priorities and helped establish the president rather than the party as the center of national elections. Roosevelt's eagerness to expand the electorate also meant that specific, narrowly construed identities were activated and that the kinds of demands made on the political system changed while the capacities of that system were less adaptable, setting

20   VOTING DELIBERATIVELY

in motion a different kind of politics, one that depended on the competing demands of interest groups. Finally, Roosevelt placed himself at the center of the election in a way that had never been done before. His campaign, divisive and at times almost demagogic, helped create a specifically personalized form of politics that replaced issues and parties with personalities and altered the content and tone of future campaigns. All these changes matter for the conduct of elections; they matter also for the conduct of our national politics.

Plan of the Book

Chapter 1: Creating Public Opinion, Muting the Public's Voice. Under Roosevelt, the Democratic National Committee (DNC) was run by Jim Farley and his aide Emil Hurja. An econometrician and White House pollster, Hurja is credited with inventing the "tracking poll."[86] His ability to predict election results was phenomenal, especially given the technology available to him.[87] He was also an important influence on policy, and Hurja may well be the motivating force behind policies like the decision to channel resources to districts with narrow majorities rather than those that had voted overwhelmingly Democratic in 1932, helping Roosevelt win reelection and exercise control over Congress.[88] Actions like this, and the understanding of public opinion that underlay those actions, had a great deal to do with the creation of a solid Democratic majority in 1936.[89] By 1935 Hurja was helping to refine what we now think of as public-opinion polling. In doing so he was also helping to redefine the idea of public opinion. Combined with the vast web of personal contacts and other forms of anecdotal evidence, the DNC under Farley thus provided the campaign with a vast and textured understanding of the national electorate. That understanding allowed Roosevelt to appeal to and mobilize the electorate in ways never before attempted. Polling was a reasonable way for the campaign to try to organize and manage an increasing large and diverse electorate. It also meant altering the ways the public and its opinions were understood and translated into policy.

Chapter 2: Empowering the Public, Privileging the Candidate. The Roosevelt campaign understood the importance of finding and organizing potential voters. These attempts are most evident in the creation of the Good Neighbor League, an ostensibly nonpartisan organization that was nonetheless dedicated to providing the White House with information about the state of the nation and the opinions of its citizens as well as supplying the campaign with a veritable army of already-organized volunteers. The administration also established a series of locally based groups under the rubric of the Committee of One, aimed at extending the national campaign into even the smallest local community. The creation of candidate-centered organizations was unprecedented and indicated the importance of early and widespread organization to electoral victory. Under Roosevelt these efforts shifted from the parties into the White House, a move that helped change the conduct of presidential campaigns and that merged the national and the local and established the president rather than the party as the center of politics in ways that had never been seen before.

Chapter 3: Mobilizing the Vote, Containing the Public. The Roosevelt White House became one of the first to constitute the electorate as what are now understood as interest groups.[90] No one had more to do with organizing and mobilizing such constituencies than Mary (Molly) W. Dewson, vice-chair of the Democratic National Committee and head of its Women's Division. The innovative mobilization tactics she pioneered illustrate the ways in which the Roosevelt campaign sought to include previously overlooked constituents. Combined with the divisions dedicated to labor and African Americans, the Women's Division also indicates some of the ways in which political hierarchies were both reinforced and altered during the New Deal as new constituencies were incorporated into existing political structures.[91] FDR expanded the electorate in ways that supported his own political goals.

Chapter 4: Speaking for the Public, Empowering the Presidency. None of these organizational innovations would have been effective, of course, without a competent candidate, and Roosevelt as a campaigner was considerably better than competent. This chapter touches on the opposition to Roosevelt in the form of Alf Landon, the Republican Party, and entities such as the Liberty League but centers on the campaign craft of Roosevelt himself, with a particular eye toward how he constructed a national constituency out of disparate groups. The chapter focuses on Roosevelt, not just because he won the election but because he put himself at the center of it. In this election Roosevelt was in many ways more important than the issues. His rhetoric gave meaning to the election, and a large part of that meaning was the argument that a strong presidential presence was the sine qua non of a strong democracy. This, as much as any of his innovations, helped change the ways we deliberate in elections and in politics more generally.

Conclusion: The Mass Public and the Presidency. The 1936 campaign exemplifies innovations in organization and offers a view into political changes that continue to affect the ways we conduct our politics and understand the mass public and its relationship to national government. The conclusion focuses on the growth of personalized politics centralized in the White House under the president's direction, the role of the mass public and public opinion as it came to be understood and measured, and the consequences of these developments for the practices of American politics into the present.

I
CREATING PUBLIC OPINION, MUTING THE PUBLIC'S VOICE

Conceptualizing and organizing public opinion is a foundational issue for democratic politics. Government in the United States has been, since "a decent respect to the opinions of mankind" served as a warrant for issuing the Declaration of Independence, firmly grounded in public opinion. But that opinion does not include all members of the polity, nor has it always been understood in the same ways. The 1936 election is fascinating not least because at that precise moment one way of understanding public opinion and the constituencies to which it attached met different, more "scientific" methods of understanding the public.[1] In the short term, traditional methods were demonstrably better able to assess the actual vote—party leader Jim Farley's prediction of the electoral vote was more accurate than that of his aide, statistician Emil Hurja—but in the long run, polling swallowed other, more anecdotal forms of surveying the public and predicting the vote and became the dominant method through which public opinion would be understood. Partly, this happened because the polity was becoming too large and too unwieldy to be comprehended in any but summary terms. Partly, it was a reflection of the fact that government officials wanted less from the public. Snapshots of approval ratings of positions on specifically delineated issues framed in narrow ways and predictions of the vote were all that the increasingly vast and complicated system could absorb. Paradoxically, then, the American mass public was increasingly incorporated into the political system and simultaneously increasingly removed from it.[2]

In 1936 Roosevelt and his aides had the benefit of a variety of sources of public opinion. These sources included open-ended data like letters from state party leaders, conversations during personal visits by members of the national party hierarchy like Jim Farley and Molly Dewson, and the correspondence from members of the clergy and the general public. Like Farley, Roosevelt had a wide correspondence. In addition, he received something on the order of five thousand to eight thousand unsolicited letters a day.[3]

Many of these letters conveyed only approval or disapproval of the president personally. Others, however, supplied detailed responses to policies, to speeches, and to other administrative actions. As the election neared, the president took this correspondence a step further and wrote to every member of the clergy in the nation, asking for their views and those of their parishioners on New Deal policies and on the state of local conditions. Between seven thousand and nine thousand people wrote back.[4] Together with the broad network of political contacts managed by Jim Farley, these letters provided Roosevelt with nuanced access to the thinking of at least some members of the mass public and those they claimed to represent.

The data available to the campaign also included more reductive data from local, state, and national newspaper polls. Hurja managed an incredible effort at quantifying public opinion, relying on what he called "trend analysis" and what we now call tracking polls, newspaper accounts, media polls, and drilling down into these data to the county and even the city level. These data provided momentary glimpses of public opinion understood in the aggregate and revealed less about the contours of public thinking and more about overall trends in the mass public's approval of FDR, a summary that fell short of indicating their vote choice or their likelihood of voting. These data were compiled and charted, and efforts within the campaign rendered them into a summary of overall public opinion on various issues. Many of these examples of public reactions to New Deal programs and to the president were the product of inconsistently worded and sporadic polling. They thus resisted tabulation and were the subject of extended memos and conversations.

Combined with the more qualitative data, though, these quantitative measures, crude though they were, gave the president and his campaign a rich, varied, and sometimes detailed understanding of the national electorate. Roosevelt's aides could track his approval rating across various issue domains, correlate it with the ways the president and his policies were being talked and written about in the states and localities, and make decisions about the causes and consequences of that approval—or lack thereof. The campaign had access to the views of opinion leaders, expressed both publicly and privately; newspaper editorials; and correspondence. They also had some access to the views of citizens through polls and from those passionate enough to write the White House. Roosevelt had at his disposal a campaign team increasingly dedicated to trying to understand public opinion expressed in a wide variety of ways.

In this chapter, I examine each of these sources of information in turn and argue that this election provides an important window into the moment when public opinion, as a measurable entity, began to displace more anecdotal forms of evidence for the mass public's response to politics and policy. That moment changed the way we understand the public as well as the ways in which political actors began to organize and mobilize it. Even in the treatment of the richer, more nuanced sources of public attitudes toward national politics there is an effort to compile, to systematize, and inevitably to reduce a bewildering array of beliefs, anecdotes, and arguments to data on which a campaign could be managed. The national government had declared itself open to the input of individuals. Paradoxically, those individuals were interesting to the government only to the extent that they could be amassed into significant numbers representing a fairly flat version of "opinion." This process neither began nor ended in 1936, but that election stands as an important intersection between campaigns that understood the public hierarchically through contacts with opinion leaders and the less hierarchically ordered emerging forms of measuring and tabulating the positions of the mass public.

This has had important consequences. As Susan Herbst has noted, for example, the possibilities for public deliberation are reduced when, rather than allowing questions and issues to emerge organically from the mass public, pollsters formulate questions to which individuals respond. Other problems arise when polls give the impressions that "the people" have spoken on a given issue, making further deliberation seem unnecessary.[5] Similarly, a collection of scholars from both political science and communication have argued that while polls have been depicted as a counter to the pervasive influence of special interests by allowing the public a voice in national politics, that may well be an overly optimistic view.[6] In short, there is good reason to believe that as a result of the changes beginning in 1936, the public became at once larger, more visible, and less able to articulate its preferences to the government.

Public Opinion and American Politics

Politicians have long sought to understand—and thus to control—public opinion. In the American context, the idea that the public, understood as a large collectivity of citizens, should have important influence over the day-to-day policy-making functions of government developed as part of the Progressive Era, with presidents like Woodrow Wilson and Theodore Roosevelt, who made explicit appeals to the public a basis for the legitimacy of their policies. It is no surprise that the "Rise of the Rhetorical Presidency," with its association with public leadership, should be traced back to these presidents.[7] Progressive reforms were not, in general, aimed at the presidency but were directed instead at ensuring mass access to the political system at the local and state level, arenas considerably more important to the nation's political life than the federal government.[8] These reforms—the recall, the referendum, and direct election of senators, for instance—were all intended to include the public in policy making. Rather than having a largely silent public assume a passive role in establishing and maintaining governmental legitimacy, during the twentieth century that public, as a mass, assumed an increasingly active role in the determination of policy.

This increasingly active role was enabled by techniques for following what was becoming referred to as "public opinion." Mass marketers in the 1920s, for instance, were ever more likely to rely on polling, although the samples were often, by contemporary standards, flawed. Using telephone directories and lists of car owners, pollsters found their respondents through means that meant they were always including specific kinds of bias in their work—only the relatively well-to-do were easily documented. Other citizens left fewer traces in public records and were harder to locate systematically. Despite this critical weakness, polling was not used only to market material goods. As the public became understood as a political resource, polling was increasingly used for political matters, large and small.[9]

Throughout the 1920s and 1930s, as Progressive politics turned into the New Deal, "science" became and remained a powerful warrant for political action. The 1925 Scopes trial, for instance, was in many ways a victory for science over religion as a way of apprehending the world and designing policies in response to that apprehension. George Gallup, the foremost defender of the scientific nature of public-opinion polls, relied on this authority and helped argue for polls as legitimate partly because they were grounded in science. Their ability to reflect empirical reality became the basis for their political legitimacy.[10] Politicians understood polls both as a reflection of political reality and as a means of creating it. Through the publication of polls, for instance, bandwagons could be created and momentum stirred.[11]

The 1930s are thus particularly interesting, for as Roosevelt sought to remake the American state, the public became one of the mechanisms through which power could be shifted from the states and localities to the federal government and, within the national government, from Congress to the presidency.[12] And while FDR was fascinated by polls, and later in his presidency used Hadley Cantril as a private White House pollster, in 1936 the White House combined intensive polling efforts with other means of calibrating public opinion, facilitating Roosevelt's endeavor to establish himself as a popular leader with legitimacy rooted in public opinion. Therein is a paradox. The mass public, increasingly a source of political legitimacy and increasingly used as a warrant for political action was, on the one hand, ever more deeply implicated in national political action. On the other hand, however, as that opinion was increasingly aggregated, individual members of the public became increasingly invisible and their opinions were increasingly flattened as their individual responses to political events and personalities were limited to the choices offered by pollsters.

In 1936 this process was still incomplete. Roosevelt, for instance, used polling data—both internal White House polls and DNC polls were routinely made available to him—and he also maintained the practice of tabulating the responses to his policies and speeches. In addition, he carried out an extensive correspondence with party leaders and others. He used press conferences to popularize the presidency and to create and maintain links with the public that depended neither on Congress nor on the party. Roosevelt engaged in multilayered ways of connecting to the public, understanding its vagaries, and orchestrating communicative campaigns designed to influence and educate it. He may have "played with public opinion as a cat with a mouse," as the editor of *Collier's* once put it, but to engage in any play at all he first had to develop an understanding of that opinion.[13] For Roosevelt, that meant relying on old means of understanding this phenomenon increasingly called "public opinion" as well as inventing new ones. In the process, he helped redefine public opinion as we understand it today.

The Particular Genius of Jim Farley

No political actor in the 1930s so typified the traditional brand of politics as Jim Farley. Not quite urban enough to become a major player in the inner councils of Tammany Hall, he nevertheless found a place in New York politics and was instrumental to Roosevelt's success in his gubernatorial races and in his first presidential bid.[14] Appointed postmaster general in the first term, Farley was in charge of patronage, a task he managed with aplomb and skill. For Farley, politics was less about the content of policy and more about the delicate balance of rewards and obligations that provided the foundation for a strong political party. His focus was organizational but his brand of politics was personal. Consequently, his correspondence was voluminous. He famously signed all his letters in green ink so as to better mark them in his correspondents' memories. He also became an early and frequent user of the new telephone technology, using phones to increase both the quantity and quality of his personal network.

Farley, like most of the politicians of his day, understood politics as a hierarchically ordered endeavor grounded in party. National party leaders worked with state party leaders who worked with heads of local party organizations. Loyalty was ensured by an elaborate structure of patronage and measured by the various leaders' ability to accurately predict and mobilize the vote.[15] Party organization was thus very personal and deeply organizational. Robert Rhea, for instance, who referred to himself as a "good Democrat," offered Farley this blunt assessment in January 1936: "If the boys want to keep their feet in the hog trough, they had better be looking around for another Democratic candidate for use in next July."[16] This correspondent received benefits from and thus was loyal to the Democratic Party and its bosses, "the boys." His loyalty to its president was much thinner. Candidates existed "for use" of party regulars and party leaders. It was a set of priorities Farley would have understood. Neither man felt the need to hide the fact that partisan loyalty entitled one to "keep their feet in the hog trough"; neither would have considered that personal loyalty to a candidate outweighed the imperatives of positioning oneself near that trough. Farley wrote, "While many criticize the spoils system, I have always felt that it is just as easy to find a good Democrat as a good Republican or vice versa and that the party in power should reward its own."[17] In Farley's world, candidates served parties who served their loyalists. Roosevelt sought to upend this balance, making the candidate the center of the party and the controller of patronage.

Under Roosevelt, then, politics were changing, and long before the enactment of McGovern-Fraser, party structures were being weakened by practices that strengthened the executive as an individual and as an institution. Facilitated, at least in part, by the rise of the mass media and enabled by the previous reforms associated with Progressivism, the parties were weakened by the growing nationalization of American politics and the kinds of organization such a politics required. As Sidney M. Milkis demonstrated, both nationalized and programmatic politics required a strong national executive controlling a strong administrative state, not a strong executive wedded to a powerful political party.[18]

These influences and practices were evident in the 1936 election. Between the convention and the general election, for example, Farley sent some 2,500 letters to local party leaders, saying, "I want the true picture" of how matters stood in their communities.[19] These leaders were contacted at least three more times during the campaign.[20] The letters he received in return averaged roughly two to five pages in length and provided detailed analyses of local political situations. Many covered congressional and senatorial races as well as the presidential election.[21] A number of these letters were pessimistic. One party leader, for instance, wrote Farley in August 1936 that he had noticed that among the criticisms gaining traction was the idea that the "Administration is carrying on an orgy of spending and incurring a tremendous public debt."[22] Such fears may have been one reason for the administration's stress during the latter stages of the campaign on the economic benefits of New Deal policies.

These letters were helpful in other ways as far as broader campaign strategy went. V. J. Dollman, for example, wrote, "At this hour Illinois is in a very doubtful state. . . . The urban vote seems reasonably secure, the farm vote is drifting away from us rapidly. Misrepresentation relative to the enormous cost of farm aid and other activities which the farmer must bear in the future has taken deep root."[23] Such information, especially when correlated with the hundreds of other letters Farley received in the late summer and early fall, would have given some clear direction about the issues the campaign most needed to address and which constituencies needed to hear which specific messages.

Farley also heard from average citizens, many of whom wrote to him with warnings and advice. One such correspondent, who chose to remain anonymous out of fear of retribution from his "bosses" and who signed himself "Just an ordinary waiter who loves the New Deal," told Farley of a conversation he overheard between two opposition senators on campaign strategy.[24] It is not clear how seriously such information was (or should have been) taken. It is clear that such letters poured into Democratic headquarters and that each one supplied at least potentially useful information on the nature of public opinion.[25]

The campaign didn't depend solely on personal letters, however. On July, 30, 1936, three days after the end of the Democratic National Convention, White House press secretary Stephen Early drafted a memo for Farley containing a copy of a Republican pamphlet titled, *Some Reasons Why the Present Administration Can and Will Be Defeated*. Early suggested that copies be sent to "appropriate officials" and that "each official should be told to go into action to counteract such propaganda."[26] The campaign grasped the necessity of rapid responses to attacks by their opponents and was quick to mobilize surrogates on the president's behalf.

Through this correspondence and through his direction of the political activities of administration officials, Farley put himself at the center of a national political organization, dedicated not to a particular program nor even to a particular candidate but to the party as an entity unto itself.[27] Importantly, in those Depression-ridden times, patronage served as the reward for loyalty to party. Supporting the New Deal and the president through loyalty to Farley paid off in terms of jobs and the ability to provide them.[28]

This brand of politics was not entirely welcome, however, and Farley also served as a lightning rod for the administration. While the president argued that he was running the country and not a campaign, Farley took unrelenting criticism on his behalf. "Day after day," Roosevelt biographer James MacGregor Burns noted, Farley "was charged with using relief funds and public funds to bribe millions of voters, with operating a colossal spoils machine, with neglecting the post office."[29] These attacks were potentially potent, for the Roosevelt coalition relied in part on the remainder of the Progressive impulse still lingering in the nation, an impulse that was strongly reformist and adamantly opposed to machine politics.[30] Farley's task was to unite the various factions of the Democratic Party while absorbing the criticism aimed at the president.[31] This task called for tact and skill and depended on the cultivation of personal relationships as well as on the distribution of political rewards and patronage. Farley was one of the nation's most adept practitioners of this brand of politics.

Despite his skill at one brand of politics, however, some of the wounds he received in 1936 were self-inflicted, a product of Farley's facility with insiders and a concomitant inability to understand how his words might resonate with a broader public. Talking to a group of Democrats in Michigan, Farley referred to Roosevelt opponent Alf Landon as the governor of a "typical prairie state," a remark that caused no small amount of uproar in critical midwestern states. "'Never use the word "typical,"' chided FDR. 'If the sentence had read "One of our splendid Prairie States," no one would have picked up on it. But the word "typical," coming from a New Yorker is meat for the opposition.'"[32] Farley knew how to talk to partisans, political insiders like himself. Roosevelt, on the other hand, had an ear carefully calibrated toward how his words would be perceived by the mass public, the individual voters on whom his political success would increasingly rely.

Campaigns, of course, are the most obvious moment when the public and public opinion may be said to matter in American politics. At no other moment is the role of public opinion so important and so visible. Given Roosevelt's mastery of the nuances of campaigning, it was perhaps natural to him to turn electoral politics into the basis of modern governance, possessing as he did an ear for the public voice. It was a voice that party officials like Farley had not been trained to hear with the same clarity FDR possessed. Farley's version of the public was as a relatively inert mass that moved at the behest of local party leaders. No one knew better than Farley how to keep those leaders under control through a carefully balanced system of rewards and punishments and how to manage them through state party leaders, who in turn answered to the national party. But a system that depended on cultivating the loyalty of millions of individuals, some of them not even members of the Democratic Party, was beyond him.

Farley was nonetheless essential to Roosevelt's 1936 campaign efforts. Facing a fractured Democratic Party, threatened by Huey Long and Townsendism on the Left and Coughlin's peculiar brand of democracy on the Right, someone had to hold the party together in the face of controversy over New Deal programs, anger at the lingering Depression, and fear caused by the changes in civic culture. Some of the burden of this task belonged to the candidate, of course, but much of it fell to Farley, his chief political aide.

Among other things, Farley was charged with keeping a close eye on Huey Long.[33] He commissioned, for instance, a secret poll for the DNC and was dismayed to find that Long and his Share the Wealth program were in fact both very popular (capable of amassing three to four million votes) and national rather than merely regional in scope. It also appeared that if Long decided to challenge Roosevelt for the presidency, FDR's opponents in the Liberty League and on Wall Street would be only too happy to subsidize that campaign, hoping to split the Democrats.[34] The White House took the threat Long posed very seriously and must have been relieved when his assassination effectively ended the challenge posed by Share the Wealth.

Farley's campaign strategy was simple and based, in large part, on the views expressed by his vast network of political contacts. First, he incorporated members of interest groups and issue-based organizations into the campaign. Second, he emphasized the economic benefits of New Deal policies. Third, he orchestrated attacks on Republican candidate Alf Landon. But more than anything else, Farley organized the election around Roosevelt and his personality, counting on the public's response to the candidate as much as to the policies he espoused.[35] Certainly, "the attitude of the President toward his own party was that of a patron, not of a slave," which would have made Farley's job difficult both in his dealings with party leaders and with the denizen of the White House.[36]

Farley's personal network provided him—and the Roosevelt campaign—with extraordinarily accurate information about the mood and behavior of the electorate. Because of its early voting, for instance, the state of Maine had been considered a bellwether of national politics—"as Maine goes," the saying went, "so goes the nation." Farley, on the basis of his massive collection of anecdotal evidence, boldly predicted that FDR would win forty-six of the forty-eight states.[37] Proved right, he quipped, "As Maine goes, so goes Vermont."[38] Farley was credited with the ability not only to predict but also therefore to control the vote—he was generally hailed as the architect of Roosevelt's victory.

Farley's own ambitions eventually collided with those of his president, and, as was so often the case with those who clashed with Roosevelt, Farley ended up an embittered opponent.[39] Historians sometimes attribute his problems to an inability to master the politics he had helped create.[40] His reliance on personal networks at a time when those networks were becoming less important as vehicles for delivering the vote meant that he would become an outsider, because party leadership depends, over everything else, on an ability to mobilize partisans. But even at the peak of his influence, Roosevelt was already widening both the electorate and his access to it.[41] The clergy letters represent the clearest and most fascinating example of this endeavor.

A New Take on the Old School

As important as Farley was, and as critical as was his ability to create support, Franklin Roosevelt was not one to leave political judgments to his staff. He had both instincts for and knowledge of politics and maintained his own network of information. In what has to be the best example of the kind of anecdotal evidence FDR sought, in September 1935 he wrote the nation's clergy a letter in which he asked for information about public reaction to specific policies and on local conditions.[42] Thousands of clergy replied, providing a wealth of detail on those conditions.[43] He thus, in Gerard Hauser's terms, opened "an epistolary public sphere."[44] These replies included comments on policy, on the politics of American culture, and on Roosevelt himself and his influence on the nation. Most movingly, they described local conditions in sometimes painful detail, sometimes including photographs so that the president could better see and understand those conditions.[45] Even when they expressed suspicion that their letters would be read, as they often did, they still seized the opportunity, however slim, of reaching the president.[46] This in itself is interesting, for the clergy seemed to well understand that Roosevelt's appeal was politically motivated and that their letters were more likely to be aggregated by staff than read by the president. Yet the opportunity to be heard, to put their congregations before the president's eyes and to influence the administration's view of the nation, was simply too important to pass up.[47]

FDR himself probably read only a very few of the letters.[48] The administration made efforts to systematize these responses, noting in a report to the president that some 120,000 letters had been delivered, and by the time the report was written, 8,294 replies had been recorded, which they believed represented the opinions of roughly 100,000 people. These opinions were summarized for the president (total favorable, 49 percent; total favorable but presenting criticism of some one or more features of New Deal programs, 33 percent; total unfavorable, 18 percent). The data were also presented in terms of approval; approval with reservations; and disapproval across issue and by state. The topics covered included, "in order of importance," liquor, works programs and relief, agriculture, and finance.[49] The twenty-eight-page report detailed the aggregated responses. There is evidence that this report received considerable attention from the White House, and the question of whether and how the letters should be made public reached the president himself.[50] These letters reveal some interesting elements in the aggregate. Far more revealing was the passion with which many of the clergy wrote.

The most heavily criticized policy was the repeal of Prohibition. Unsurprisingly, the clergy were opposed to the "liquor traffic" and all the social ills they associated with it. More than 1,700 letters included criticism of Repeal.[51] One clergyman wrote wrathfully, "You pledged the nation repeal and we have repeal. We also have one hell of a mess. I suppose you are proud of your achievement when you read or hear of some one [sic], perhaps a child, being killed by a drunken driver."[52] Others, less willing to blame the president, remained critical of "the return of liquor, which has filled our streets, subways, and buildings with reeling 'drunks.'"[53] The clergy were most concerned about the effects of Repeal and blamed many of the social ills they saw on the liquor traffic and sometimes also on the president who authorized that traffic. It was clear in these letters that cultural changes, at work at least since the 1920s, were, in the context of the Depression, causing the clergy significant concern. Roosevelt may have noted this concern but it is doubtful that he gave Repeal much thought.

The anger aroused by the Agricultural Assistance Administration was far more worrying from the administration's perspective. The point of this program was to provide, through proper planning, a balance between agricultural production and consumption and thus to stabilize farm prices.[54] Initially, this meant the destruction of crops and the killing of farm animals, mostly pigs. The destruction of food in the midst of widespread want drove the clergy (and many other Americans) to distraction.[55] The clergy considered the program "unsound and morally undefensible [sic]."[56] Virtually none of the letters favored the Agricultural Adjustment Act, although there was support for the New Deal's efforts to help farmers. From this, FDR could have learned to stress relief for farmers and to avoid defending the means he was using to achieve it.

The animus concerning cultural change revealed itself in other ways as well, especially in the clergy's discussion of the National Recovery Administration.[57] The NRA seemed to symbolize for many Americans the problems associated with relying for political advice on a well-educated but naive staff of "Brain Trusters."[58] As Lewis L. Gould notes, under Roosevelt, presidential advisers became celebrities in their own right, a development that not all citizens appreciated.[59] "Members of the Brain Trust were charged with subscribing to practically all alien 'isms' except cannibalism and of following virtually every foreign ruler except Haile Selassie."[60] One minister displayed this ambivalence, writing, "I think the individual critics and enemies of the socalled [sic] brain cabinet is the chief source of a lot of anti-propaganda. It has been evident for a long time that a big industrialist or a great professor cannot, in the first place, separate himself from his personal interests, and in the latter case from his theory and philosophy."[61] It is not clear from this letter whether the author supported the Brain Trust or not. Surely he saw them as an example of the ways in which New Deal critics were obtaining leverage over public opinion. Elvin Lim has noted an increasing anti-intellectualism in presidential rhetoric.[62] There is good evidence that this anti-intellectual bias was pervasive in the United States during Roosevelt's time in office. Arthur M. Schlesinger Jr., for example, quoted Maury Maverick (D-TX), who underlined the nation's pervasive anti-intellectualism: "'Stop!' I shouted. 'Don't tell me. Whenever you use a word I don't understand it makes me mad. I am an American! The word nodule is not understood by the American people nor is it understood by me, which makes it worse—and I do not want to understand what it means. No one wants to listen to your academic phrases.'"[63] Members of Congress and the mass public were suspicious, not only of words like "nodule," but of the ways in which those comfortable with such words were changing American politics. They worried about a national state grounded in "theory," not least because such states, like the communist Soviet Union and fascist Germany, seemed increasingly on the rise internationally and prone to the destruction of human freedom. Theory, and those comfortable with it, seemed threatening on a variety of fronts, foreign and domestic.

The perceived threat behind other cultural trends was also made clear by the clergy. They worried that relief without work was detrimental to American morality and fretted over the potential for government programs to help the "undeserving" as well as the "deserving" poor. D. W. Hawkins, for example, wrote, "The 'Dole System' of the last year has done more harm than good, many able bodied men have learned to look to the government for daily bread and they have fallen in love with the system. . . . To be sure, all of us alike believe in taking care of the dependent, the crippled and the helpless, but to encourage this among the able-bodied is dangerous indeed."[64] Others were less generous. A minister from Georgia, for example, wrote, "A great many of the underprivileged people are in reality like submarginal land, not fit for cultivation. No program for the underprivileged can be justified which does not in wisdom and justice to all concerned seek to discriminate between individuals and families which are able though underprivileged, and those who are submarginal and inferior."[65] Many among the clergy were more compassionate than these writers, but there was considerable concern even among those most strongly in support of the Works Progress Administration that it could undermine the nation's work ethic.[66] Specifically, they feared not only that the undeserving poor might benefit but also that the projects were more likely to produce various forms of boondoggling than anything of real benefit.[67] And many worried about corruption and feared that the programs were being used to political advantage.[68]

Nonetheless, the clergy realized the importance of protecting the nation's neediest citizens and endorsed, often in glowing terms, the new Social Security legislation.[69] "The Social Security Act is a 'Good Neighbor' deed, done in the spirit of the 'Good Samaritan.' It is commendable in its aim," wrote one.[70] Another referred to it as "the truest answer to the problems made by any nation at any time in the history of the world."[71] Despite the generally positive responses to Social Security, many of them favored the Townsend Plan, and others warned Roosevelt of its impending threat to his administration, fearing that its adherents were "steadily gaining ground and will be an important factor in the next election, their plans if carried out will bankrupt the nation."[72] Thus, for some at least, Roosevelt appeared to occupy a moderate position, offering protection for the vulnerable without unduly risking the overall stability of the political system. There was concern about the consequences of his policies to be sure, but many found those consequences less worrisome than the alternatives on either the Right or the Left. These letters also reveal the nuances of their support for and opposition to the New Deal; rarely could these reactions be adequately understood through summary data.

Such data, for instance, entirely omits the very real emotion in these letters. Even at this distance, the pain of those who pled for attention to the African Americans, American Indians, Mexican Americans, and other marginalized groups on whom a disproportionate share of economic deprivation had fallen is evident.[73] Rev. Glenn B. Coyenkill, for instance, noted the deprivation of "our Western New York Indians," stating that "all that many of them have is the land they live on." He argued, "A single tractor, properly placed, could do much to take care of many garden plots and the expense would be trifling."[74] Despite the agonizing need, it is doubtful than the Indians got that tractor or, indeed, any other form of real assistance from Washington.[75]

One correspondent angrily pointed to the starkest effects of racial inequalities: "In some states, in this nation, the most humble citizen, The Forgotten Man, has very little protection. . . . He is murdered, burned, shot down, hanged, for the merest trifle. The so-called courts of justice, in many instances, are nothing but legalized mobs; no one seeks to find out or punish the guilty party. . . . Why not take a stand and tell congress that the Antilynching Bill must be passed before any other legislation shall be considered."[76] Such pleas for national help to solve local problems were among the thorniest of issues for the administration.[77] In the case of African Americans, those pleas generally went unanswered.

Despite the occasional requests on behalf of the disenfranchised, however, in general, the clergy warned Roosevelt not to go too far or proceed to quickly on social matters. He was censored for fishing and holding cabinet meetings on Sunday, for the divorces and multiple marriages of his children, and in general for failing his duty as an exemplar of proper morality.[78] When the clergy spoke of gender issues, it was to insist that married women be denied jobs to maintain the employment of men. "Never should it be allowed in such time as this, that a man hold's [sic] a job and his wife also has a fat job, this means teachers, preachers, any one."[79] These criticisms were plentiful and often acerbic despite the fact that New Deal programs generally acceded to rather than challenged nationally prevalent assumptions about gender, marriage, and class.[80] The clergy tended to believe, with George H. Schuster, that "the same selfishness and greed that plunged us into this depression is still in evidence everywhere. . . . What this country needs is a national regeneration."[81] They wanted the president to call the nation into a day of prayer, to live a more godly life himself, and to encourage devotion among his constituents. The Reverend R. D. Robeson, for instance, contented himself with answering the president's letter by writing across the text of that letter, "Call the nation back to God w/ prayer," and mailing it back to the White House.[82]

As these examples indicate, the clergy, invited by the president to offer their thoughts on the direction of national policy, weighed in on a wide variety of issues from diverse perspectives. They provided a window in the world as it was experienced by everyday Americans in all its richness, humor, and pathos. Such letters provided the White House with a deeper and more textured understanding of the mass public than was attainable through any scientific methods. But the increasing influence of such scientific methods was not lost on members of the Roosevelt administration. Even as they reached for anecdotal evidence about the nation, they also sought to systematize and quantify the information they received. Without such aggregation, there was simply too much of it to be digested, absorbed, and put to use. No one had more to do with systematizing and quantifying public opinion in 1936 than Emil Hurja.

Quantifying Public Opinion

Before there was Nate Silver there was Emil Hurja. Known as "the crystal gazer from Crystal Falls," in Jim Farley's phrase, and more popularly as the "Wizard of Washington," Hurja's innovations moved the study of public opinion into the realm of science rather than anecdote, guesswork, and political instinct. He told his assistants, for example, that "politics is a matter of geography plus economics. There isn't any magic in this; it's work."[83] For Hurja, public opinion was amenable to objective testing. All one needed was access to a large enough sample and the right tools for understanding what that sample revealed. He was considered so successful, in fact, that citizens wrote to him asking for election predictions "for wagering purposes."[84] Hurja's innovations may or may not have won many bets, but they changed the way Americans conduct political campaigns and the ways both the public and its opinions are understood.

Hurja's 1936 polling operation was extensive if, by contemporary standards, crude. In the files of the Roosevelt Library, for instance, there are complete state-by-state election forecasts, which include polls and notes from party and opinion leaders in the various states offering their opinions on whether FDR would carry their state and, if so, by how much.[85] Farley relied on the anecdotal evidence in these notes for his prediction. Hurja depended on the quantifiable data. Hurja also polled opinion of Roosevelt's speeches and policies and ran polls on his potential opponents. The Roosevelt campaign had more complete and varied sources of information on the public and its opinions than any administration or campaign in history up to that time.

Hurja, like the better-known George Gallup, worked at a time when the old, instinct-based forms of political prediction were giving way to scientifically inflected means of understanding public opinion.[86] Prior to the advent of polling, political actors relied on local party leaders, editorials, and other informal but hierarchically structured means of political analysis and prediction. Hurja—and Roosevelt—saw in these new techniques a way to systematize and organize an increasingly complicated and sprawling national electorate.[87] The broader and more inclusive the electorate became, the more important such methods also became. Unlike the clergy letters, which gave poignancy and depth to the opinions they expressed and which allowed interlocutors to name and order their own beliefs, polling not only erased emotional intensity but reduced the range of opinions with which the campaign was concerned. No one can reply to a poll with an argument or include a nuance on an opinion. Polling encourages a democratic understanding of politics—it represents, through sampling, a broad swath of the public in which all individuals are theoretically treated as equal. At the same time, it aggregates something called "opinion," but in doing so it creates a flattened version of that opinion.[88]

In 1936 polling served to redefine the public as well. Columnist Arthur Krock wrote, "Two of the four groups which will probably decide the election have hardly been sampled, if at all. These four groups are the new voters, the colored [sic] voters, labor and agrarian citizens; and it is doubtful whether it will be possible to produce an accurate representation of the first two mentioned. This is because their names are not so easily come by in the public records."[89] Even knowing that a large number of people were invisible to pollsters, pundits and politicians treated poll evidence as definitive. Krock, for instance, concluded that column with a prediction of a close election, a prediction based on the polling data he understood as flawed.

Hurja was dedicated to the endeavor of capturing and quantifying political reality. Not only did he conduct his own polls, but he was a voracious collector of all kinds of data. His files are full of newspaper clippings; registration data; maps of radio stations and their locations; comparisons of congressional votes by district, across issues, over time; county data; and city data. If any information out there could help understand public opinion, Hurja collected it.[90] He tracked Roosevelt's popularity across poll and over time, calculated breakdowns in county votes, created charts rating the importance of various states in various polls, and compiled records of registration rules by state.[91] The campaign also sent letters asking about the rules governing straight-ticket voting, previous totals for registered voters, and current totals of registered voters by party.[92] It is abundantly clear that Hurja was making systematic attempts to understand and measure public opinion, the vote, and the relationship between the two.

His polling indicated, with relative precision, the limits of the Democratic coalition in its contemporaneous form. Such polls, for example, made it clear that despite the vote in the previous national election, many Republicans had by no means converted to the Democratic cause but were reacting to the "hard times" and blaming Herbert Hoover for them.[93] Hurja also tracked Roosevelt's popularity by media poll (*Literary Digest, National Inquirer*, etc.) across time, so he had a reasonably precise understanding of where the president stood with the public. This meant that he could compare data about previous voting patterns with the data on the president's popularity at any given point. He could do this at the state, congressional-district, and county level. There is evidence that he was working on ways to correct the national data with reference to these patterns at the local level. And he was doing the math by hand—the files are full of scraps of paper covered with scribbled calculations.

This wasn't statistics for its own sake but was driven by electoral concerns. Consistent with Farley's emphasis on the importance of electoral organization, Hurja's files contain details about registration rules by party and across states, including dates and limits on registration, material clearly important in mobilizing the Roosevelt vote.[94] The DNC took these data seriously. They also went to great lengths to attain it—they wrote, for example to the clerks in every city visited on the campaign's Western Tour, requesting data on the 1932 vote totals so they could be compared to projections for 1936.[95] Hurja's files at the Library of Congress contain detailed letters from state party leaders and candidates.[96] Both the amount of data and the burdens of processing those data by hand are astounding. The level of knowledge that this effort would have supplied the campaign and its candidate was equally significant. Hurja sought to understand the public, not for its own sake, but so the knowledge could be applied to the narrow end of reelecting the president. This meant that the means of gaining that understanding and the understanding itself were subordinated to and circumscribed by the electoral goal. The public became, for Hurja, the electorate. Its members were those who could be captured by voting roles and its opinions those that would become a valence in deciding vote choice.

Electorally driven, Hurja's polling had consequences that went beyond the election. Because he could claim detailed knowledge of the public's response to administration policy, Hurja influenced the ways in which the administration communicated about that policy. In October 1936, for example, he suggested comparing the results of the Works Progress Administration to those of various other industries as a way of arguing for its comparative efficiency.[97] Of course, polling was being increasingly done across the nation and in a variety of venues, and the administration amassed polling data from a wide variety of sources, keeping careful track of the quantitative data and what it might mean for administration policy making.[98]

These data weren't just in the form of polls. Hurja, for example, created beautifully colored charts, locating the individual members of Congress, by delegation, in terms of how they voted on key administration initiatives. One could, at a glance, gain a good understanding of the geographic voting on specific issues; that these charts were collected into one bundle meant that patterns were easily discernible. Given the administration's focus on patronage, these data are likely to have had both symbolic and very material consequences.[99]

The White House didn't overlook other kinds of data in favor of polls. As noted earlier, Jim Farley maintained an extensive personal and political correspondence, writing hundreds of letters a week. Both polling evidence and more anecdotal kinds of evidence—editorials and personal accounts—appear throughout the speechwriter files, indicating that they served as an inventional resource for those crafting FDR's campaign and that the administration relied on anecdotal as well as statistical evidence in constructing its understanding of public opinion.[100] The public was significantly enlarged during the Roosevelt years and became more diverse and complex as a result. As FDR grounded claims to political legitimacy in the "will of the people," capturing a workable conception of that will became increasingly important and difficult task. Public opinion didn't just have to be captured, however. It also needed to be distilled into a form that could serve as a useful guide for an increasingly vast government. Depth and nuance were sacrificed so that public opinion could be used to inform and legitimate public action. These processes began during elections and were informed by electoral logics. They also facilitated the permanent campaign and strengthened the hand of the president in national policy making by emphasizing the president's relationship with the mass public.

Conclusion

Even though Farley's prediction of the outcome was more accurate than Hurja's—or Roosevelt's—the shift from party-driven to candidate-driven politics and the increasing emphasis on quantifiable measures of public opinion and voter behavior were clearly on display in the 1936 election. Roosevelt himself noted it: "There was something terrible about the crowds that lined the streets, Roosevelt remarked to Ickes—he could hear them crying out, 'He saved my home,' 'He gave me a job.'"[101] That the public understood the president rather than the government or the party to be the source of their salvation speaks volumes about the political changes of the era. This reliance on FDR as an individual facilitated his efforts, as Milkis so convincingly argues, "not to rouse public opinion but to teach the American people a new public philosophy, albeit one that promised to reinvigorate the Framers' understanding of the social contract." Those efforts, instantiated in the New Deal and in the American state it profoundly changed, have had a lasting impact on national politics in the United States. These changes diminished the role of political parties in favor of other forms of political organization.[102] Somewhat perversely, 1936 stands as a clear example of FDR's willingness to build "a party to end partisanship."[103] Roosevelt stressed public opinion and his personal relationship with the public to free himself from the influence of the party bosses and the dictates of party organization.

These efforts were in general wildly successful (the problems caused by court packing and the purge were exceptions to this rule; they were also exceptions to Roosevelt's sensitivity to public opinion). Roosevelt's political career depended on an understanding of what was politically possible given the nature and structure of public opinion. In developing that understanding, Roosevelt and his campaign had at their disposal nuanced and varied sources of that opinion. Ranging from the personal contacts and private information Farley depended on through the more statistically based analysis pioneered by his aide Emil Hurja and the detailed responses of the American clergy to the policies and practices of the New Deal, Roosevelt's information was national in scope and local in orientation.

Political parties had historically served to organize public opinion in the United States. Under Roosevelt, those parties were undermined and new forms of organization and mobilization had to be invented and implemented. The 1936 election thus served, in Milkis's terms, as part of a "surrogate constitutional convention," making the nation in some ways more democratic but also providing new constraints on the president and the government that was increasingly centered on him.[104] As the public grew and diversified, its opinions were increasingly important as guides and warrants for governmental action. At the same time, these opinions were rendered into forms useful to the government, flattening complicated opinions into simplified forms and erasing the complexities of individual responses to government.

2

EMPOWERING THE PUBLIC, PRIVILEGING THE CANDIDATE

Much of FDR's political success can be attributed to his organizational skill. He was, famously, a rather chaotic administrator and often frustrated those around him. But he was adept at devising organizational structures deigned to work his will through a government poorly designed for presidential control. He was equally skillful at adapting campaign structures to work his will through an organization poorly designed to respond to candidates rather than party imperatives. In both environments the key was the ways in which the structures facilitated Roosevelt's personal brand of leadership. Roosevelt was as willing to invent and operate through structures that allowed him to circumvent political and governmental routines as to operate within those routines. Jim Farley, for example, noted that the president was interested in organizing the public along extrapartisan lines and traced the origins of what he referred to as the "different committees" to a conversation he had with FDR in January 1936. In that conversation, the two discussed the development of extrapartisan committees with titles such as Friends of Roosevelt, the Good Neighbor League (GNL), the Roosevelt Republican League, and the Committee of One (CO).[1] The creation of these committees indicates the extent to which FDR was willing to find inventive means of capturing the public and also that his thinking was not confined to party. They also indicate his willingness to create political entities that answered to the candidate, weakening the parties' increasingly tenuous hold on national politics and beginning what we now call "candidate-centered politics."

Candidate-centered politics offer a kind of false inclusiveness, in which the people's will is understood to be enacted through the person rather than a set of practices or procedures, focusing attention on the character of political actors rather than on the institutions through which they operate.[2] On the one hand, FDR's extrapartisan organizations promulgated the kind of increased inclusiveness favored by scholars of deliberative democracy.[3] Certainly, they allow us to look at the way members of such organizations enacted citizenship in a particular context and to examine the kinds of practical reasoning they practiced.[4] On the other hand, these organizations made the election of a candidate their prime concern, flattening and narrowing the purposes of participation and locating political agency in the candidate.

As the 1936 election neared, FDR was increasingly looking for ways to supplement party organizations. He sought to create and foster a coalition, not just a strong Democratic Party. To do so he was willing to look to extrapartisan ways of organizing and mobilizing the vote. This effort undoubtedly helped bring new voters into the political system on the basis of their loyalty to the president and to his policies. Voters in the New Deal coalition, then, looked first to the president and then to party. Both still mattered; Roosevelt was happy to engage in party-building activities and worked hard to strengthen the Democratic Party. But by 1936 the balance between president and party began to shift and the creation of nonparty campaign organizations was an important aspect of that process.

The organization and constituencies of these groups differed but the principle behind them was the same: the creation of a vast network of individuals, acting on the basis of their own belief in the administration and its policies, actively recruiting others to the cause. The theory was that individuals were the most effective means of communicating the New Deal message to other individuals. These organizational efforts made no effort to transcend or circumvent party. They worked alongside it. As with Roosevelt's adaptation of polling, he did not seek here to displace current political practices but to add to them. Here, as in other ways, 1936 represented a moment when Roosevelt had the best of both worlds: a relatively strong party organization cooperating with other forms of organizing and mobilizing the mass public. Parties are traditionally the mechanism for forming, in Sidney M. Milkis's words, "bonds of civic affiliation."[5] Through these organizations Roosevelt and his campaign facilitated extrapartisan means for encouraging such bonds. Importantly, these organizations tied them to the person of the president, not to the political party.

Attaching civic affiliation to individuals thins those ties in ways that are not similarly true for organizational affiliations. Mobilization through extrapartisan organizations was effective in the short term but was not intended to outlast a particular election cycle.

Such forms of extrapartisan organization, rooted in earlier reform movements, were fairly prevalent in the 1930s and into the 1940s. Roosevelt had his various committees and the Republicans had the American Liberty League.[6] Later, in the midst of the Great Debate over American intervention, the Committee to Defend America by Aiding the Allies (the White Committee) faced off against America First, dedicated to the isolationist cause. These committees and their ubiquity on the American political scene were evidence of three important trends, all of which were clear in the 1936 election. First, the Roosevelt realignment was underway, but the final lines of that coalition would not be fully drawn until after the argument over the degree and extent of American intervention in World War II was essentially ended by passage of Lend-Lease in January 1941.[7] As with all realignments, this meant that while it was in process, divisions along party lines were fluid and shifting, the number of independents was rising, and partisan affiliations were weakened.[8] In this environment extrapartisan committees and organizations facilitated political participation, especially among those whose partisan allegiance was shifting.

But that participation caused concerns of its own. The 1934 midterm elections indicated that the Democrats were increasing their strength in the urban North and the commercial West. Both of these developments unsettled the party's traditional southern, rural base almost as much as it worried the Republicans.[9] The North and West were full of new immigrants, people of color, and "foreign types." The question of what these people might do with political power and the ends to which such power might be put, were matters of grave concern to the older, more traditional constituencies who had long held power as a matter of demographic right. Existing party structures seemed unable to contain, much less to control, these new and somewhat threatening elements of an increasingly sprawling national electorate.[10] Extrapartisan committees were one mechanism that might both facilitate political participation and control it; these new people might have a role in the election, but party power was reserved for traditional leaders. It is notable, for instance, that the Democrats decided in 1935 to refuse any contribution over $1000, hoping to open up access to the government to the many and clearly signaling that theirs was not a campaign dedicated to the interests of the few.[11] It is equally significant that in all of the

Roosevelt administration's organizational efforts, one of the key elements was concern for finding ways to bridge the urban-rural divide. It was imperative for the nation to find ways to reconcile the old nation with the emerging one.[12]

Second, at the same time that these organizations supplemented political parties, they also contributed to the weakening of party structures. Organizations such as the Liberty League and the Committee of One were specifically designed to be nonpartisan and to organize public opinion (and thus the behavior of the mass public) in ways that coincidentally subverted the traditional parties. These organizations did not offer patronage as rewards for loyalty. Like the organizations most often associated with Progressive Era activists, the rewards were ideological or policy based.[13] The attachments formed by organizations like the GNL were to the person of the president. They were likely to transmute themselves into partisan attachments only to the extent that the party was understood as synonymous with the president and the president's program.

This candidate-centered element allowed for the third characteristic of these organizations: they were both national and local. They thus could compete directly with political parties as organizational mechanisms. Both the GNL and the CO, like other extrapartisan organizations of the period, were initiated at the national level, often by the national party. But the emphasis was clearly and specifically on the local. The issues these organizations focused their attention on were decided by the national government—taxes, foreign policy, and so on. The discussions themselves were held in communities, among individuals. The point was to encourage individual allegiance to the national program through interpersonal contact. National policies were understood through their effects on local communities.

These organizations mirrored political parties in all but one important respect. Political parties had local organizations run by local bosses who managed local patronage. There was a loose hierarchy and an element of organizational discipline. Organizations like the GNL and CO were not really organizations at all. They were loose affiliations of like-minded individuals who were informally connected through common allegiance to similar principles. There were no local bosses, no patronage, and no kind of discipline. They thus encouraged, but could not enforce, certain kinds of political behavior. And they were designed to be temporary—they lasted only as long as the policy or electoral campaign required them. Unlike parties, they had no long-term organizational imperatives.

In all these characteristics, these committees, originated as supplements to the party organizations, also helped to organize the public in ways inconsistent with the continued health of political parties.[14] Rather than a strong party government, Roosevelt organized a governing coalition—a very different entity indeed. These organizations facilitated locally based forms of deliberation. The GNL and the CO encouraged discussions of a variety of national issues among people who had previously been largely left out of the national conversation. They thus clearly facilitated political participation among parts of the national polity. They also encouraged increased demands on a political system not designed to accommodate such demands and tended to narrow the focus of that system to the office of the president and the executive branch. These processes were readily apparent in the 1936 election and were developed in response to the political context of the 1930s.

The Political Context

One of the important elements in the context surrounding the creation of Roosevelt's extrapartisan organizations was the generalized politics of intolerance that characterized the 1930s.[15] The nation was divided between urban and rural, rich and poor; it split along religious lines; the continued economic woes facilitated the rise of radicalism on both the Left and the Right.[16] Roosevelt, whose interest was in reforming rather than revolutionizing the system, steered a difficult and at times erratic course between those who wanted him to enact sweeping changes and those who balked at any change at all. As 1935 turned into 1936, the noise appeared to get louder, threatening to drown the voices of moderation. Republicans, Democrats, Townsendites, communists, socialists, anti-Semites, racists, and fascists all organized during these years, with varying levels of success.

Attempting to govern amid the cacophony, Roosevelt sought ways to conciliate enough of the public to maintain a moderate course and provide for governmental stability.[17] The Democratic Party was part of this strategy, of course. Roosevelt campaigned as a Democrat and for other Democrats as well. It was also important to capture the votes of those unwilling to commit to the party but willing to commit to the leadership of this particular candidate. In seeking those votes, the president looked for extrapartisan means of political organization. These organizations did not have to be as broad in membership as political parties; they could be as narrow as necessary to accomplish their ends. Since they were not advancing candidates for office, they did not have to consider electoral imperatives. They existed to bridge particular kinds of gaps in the mass public and in doing so to organize the public for a Roosevelt victory.

Religious difference represented one of the most intractable sites of division. Anti-Semitism was a national problem, and it represented a particularly difficult one for Roosevelt, as his administration was often "accused" of having too strong a Jewish influence. In some circles Roosevelt's programs were referred to as the "Jew Deal."[18] Catholics, upset by the anticlericalism in Mexico and the recognition of the Soviet Union, also presented a coalitional challenge.[19] Many Catholics lived in the urban Northeast, and Catholic enclaves were among the immigrant populations of most major cities. Father Coughlin's support in 1932 had helped win many of these parishioners to the Roosevelt cause. If he was going to keep their votes, FDR had to find ways to reconcile their interests with those of the rest of his coalition.[20]

Race represented another problem for Roosevelt, as the influence of southern Democrats prevented him from pursuing more equitable racial policies. But the nation's economic problems, more severe in the South than elsewhere, also meant that poor blacks bore the brunt of the Depression and suffered from increased violence at the hands of poor whites.[21] Roosevelt deplored such violence but did little to actively prevent it. He refused to work for the antilynching bill and signed no major civil rights legislation.[22] The administration was better at responding to organized pressure than to moral demands, and African Americans were too weak politically to provide enough such pressure to overcome the demands of southern Democrats and the inertia of northern whites.[23] Despite the administration's inaction, northern blacks increasingly left the Republicans to vote Democratic, a move that was premised on the potential economic benefits of the New Deal rather than on any belief in its commitment to racial equality.[24] But race, like religion, remained a problem for Roosevelt, for he needed to accommodate both northern blacks and southern Democrats, as he needed to accommodate Protestants, Catholics, and Jews to keep his electoral coalition intact.

One way to do this was to understand these divisions in terms of another one. Roosevelt faced an increasing rural-urban divide, in which "old stock" Americans who remained in the nation's rural pockets and newer immigrants, blacks, and a younger urban population found less and less common ground.[25]

Both the form of politics (urban machines) and the culture of the city (symbolized for many by the return of the saloon) threatened rural citizens, many of whom were forced off the land and into strange new environments in urban centers throughout the Midwest and into California. The distance between *The Great Gatsby* and *The Grapes of Wrath* seemed unbridgeable.

But to this president, no political distance was ever unbridgeable. FDR consistently rejected the idea that American politics were characterized by permanent classes; politics were for him remarkably fluid, in constant need of adjustment.[26] This meant that the middle ground was often found in process rather than in policy.[27] For him, politics was a matter of balancing interests. He understood his job as that of a broker among and between these interests. Almost all political interests and affiliations were to be understood as legitimate, but not all would be rewarded with policy in the short term and even those who got some of what they wanted rarely got all their demands answered. Some would have to settle for legitimacy and recognition. Continued loyalty had the potential for continued incremental policy achievement but it was no guarantee.

Throughout the 1930s, while FDR did little in terms of combating organized opposition on the Right, he also did not oppose the formation of groups on the Left, regarding American socialism and communism with bemusement rather than repression (that would come later).[28] Instead he sought to strengthen the middle.[29] Roosevelt seemed to take the position that if the center held, the fringes could do no lasting harm, and he appeared to regard no group as able to seriously threaten American political life. He offered almost no overt challenges to any of the proliferation of organizations and tolerated the German American Bund, the Klan, and the Communist Party alike. He approached the task of strengthening the center in the face of increasingly vocal pressure from the Right and Left in a variety of ways. The one that concerns me here is the development of extraparty organizations, designed to find and strengthen the middle ground, often at the expense of a few well-chosen enemies.[30] Interestingly, those enemies were rarely actual extremists; they were more likely to be those near enough to the center to challenge his own position as national arbiter. Such threats he disposed of by associating them with the fringe, a tactic that both widened the center itself and put him indisputably at the heart of it. These organizations thus facilitated national conversations on issues and, by making it clear that the national government should be empowered to address those issues through the intervention of a strong president, also increased the demands on the system and narrowed perceptions of it to focus on the chief executive.

The Good Neighbor League

Political parties are important not least because they serve as vast organizing and consensus-building institutions. By virtue of their task of nominating and electing national and local public officials, parties must seek common ground and must endeavor to find ways to reconcile a variety of often competing interests. Roosevelt, of course, was both aware of this function and happy to work within the boundaries of party for some purposes. He was also happy to find ways to supplement the party and even occasionally happy to subvert it to advance his own programmatic goals. The 1934 midterm elections had seemed to prove the dominance of the Democratic Party. The sharp decline in Roosevelt's personal popularity since those elections, however, made relying on the party alone a risky endeavor, because of the internal elements opposed to his leadership. So the Roosevelt campaign looked for other ways of organizing the electorate and ensuring the president's reelection. These extrapartisan organizations did not operate separately from FDR. They were, in fact, explicitly connected to his reelection efforts. But they were also explicitly disconnected from partisan efforts to ensure that reelection. They were organized primarily around the president and did not work for the election of other Democrats.

FDR established the Good Neighbor League under the leadership of Charles Stelzle. The GNL was, in the terms offered by the director of its Speakers' Bureau, both nonpartisan and explicitly dedicated to Roosevelt's reelection.[31] Within two and half years of its founding, the league claimed membership of "30,000 leaders in local communities who may be called upon for service in connection with special events, or during certain periods."[32] It operated in some two thousand cities and towns within the forty-eight states.[33] Open to all American citizens of voting age who believed "that the Principle of the Good Neighbor is an expression of the American ideal and should be made a fundamental policy of the American Government," the GNL flourished during the early days of the New Deal and played a significant role in the 1936 election. There were no dues, but members were entitled to an enrollment certificate and membership button. They also received literature, "free of charge . . . for your own use and distribution."[34] The organizers of the GNL understood the power of interpersonal campaign communication: the idea was to find those motivated enough to join and to use them to motivate others of their acquaintance.[35] The actual work required by the national organization and its leaders was minimal. Most of the work of grassroots organizing was done at the local level and by private individuals at virtually no cost to the GNL's national organization.

Interestingly, the idea that a nonpartisan organization might do more good than a partisan one, at least in some parts of the country, was fairly pervasive. Herbert Gaston, for instance, wrote to Henry Morgenthau at the Treasury Department to suggest that "in the cities and towns" of Minnesota there was "much the same intensity of feeling against the administration as in the East." That animosity could be "best neutralized, I think, by a non-partisan Roosevelt-for-President" organization in the Northwest. It should have a strong LaFollette Progressive and Farmer-Labor slant. We can't carry these states on an appeal to support the Democratic party [sic] and a Democratic organization."[36] The author noted here the relative importance of the candidate and the party in Roosevelt's reelection campaign, and the candidate clearly trumped the party. Note that the author of this letter distinguished between the president, the Democratic Party, and the administration. These disconnections were somewhat more startling at that time than they might appear to us now. Because it was increasingly possible to carve up politics this way in 1936, however, FDR capitalized on such distinctions to rely on locally legitimate leaders—from outside his party and his administration and supposedly free of its political motivations—to extend their legitimacy to him personally. Extrapartisan organizations were not just ancillary to partisan efforts. They were important in their own right and provided a specific kind of legitimacy and authority to the Roosevelt campaign.

Recruitment of members focused on labor leaders, clergymen, and educators.[37] These groups, of course, represented the elite of most local communities and also constituted the opinion leaders of those communities. The GNL reached for those most likely to have broad networks of personal relationships. Through them, the GNL could reach the maximum number of voters with the minimum effort. This also expanded the GNL's reach. Avowedly nonpartisan, the GNL could extend its tentacles into neighborhoods, other civic organizations, and individuals whose personal networks included independents, undecided voters, and even conservatives as well as the Democratic Party faithful. New Deal and pro-Roosevelt information was thus made widely available and even found its way into opposition enclaves.

This infiltration of the enemy camp was made easier by the fact that officially, the GNL sought to improve relations with business and to create good will between "Rural and Urban populations" and among "foreign-speaking populations and native Americans, Jews and gentiles, Capital and Labor." The league paid particular attention to what it deemed "the necessity" of "the breaking down of racial and religious prejudices" and hoped to do so through an information campaign consisting of conferences, newsletters, and the production of research on economic and social problems.[38]

The GNL understood as its mission the reconciliation of specific kinds of national divisions—the administration, presumably, or someone within it, identified region, immigration, religion, and class distinctions as integral to the prevailing structures of American politics and set out to transcend those divisions. In doing so, it aimed at reconstituting American politics.[39] Their success in this endeavor is indisputable. The GNL also relied on education as persuasion, offering research, conferences, newsletters, and all kinds of information. The league thus enacted a particular kind of leadership, based on the notion that democracy depended on an informed citizenry and that all the nation's citizens were capable of being informed. Access to government, this approach implied, did not depend on access to formal education. It was not reserved for elites. All citizens could inform themselves about policy and governmental action and could make wise choices based on that information. The GNL thus actively encouraged citizens to learn about, discuss, and participate in politics. Its explicit message was that government was open to all. This tactic reflected the arguments behind the New Deal, underlining its potential to represent and its promise to remember the "forgotten man." Here, as elsewhere during the election, the vehicle for representation and remembrance was explicitly the government and implicitly the president, not the party.

The pamphlet *Don't You Want This Kind of an America?* advertised the Good Neighbor League by noting that the first element of the ideal nation was that it "makes human values the first concern of government." The text defined "the state" as "the duly constituted representative of an organized society of human beings—created by them for their mutual protection and well-being." Other elements of the ideal nation included defining patriotism "in terms of people"; seeking both social justice and peace; proclaiming itself "at war against poverty"; and endeavoring to make a world "safe for the home-makers." The ideal nation also "safeguards childhood" and is "concerned for morale as well as for money."[40] It was a nation of mutually dependent neighbors, united by a shared commitment to spiritual values. This description evoked both nostalgia and hope and offered a vision of a nation that was not reeling from the effects of the Depression but was vital and active and looking forward to the future. Citizens needed merely to be mobilized for electoral action to secure that future. This rhetoric encouraged citizens to believe that they had a stake in the government and that they could look to that government for security and social justice.

Specifically, the GNL indicated it was driven by policy concerns and that citizens, too, should be focused on the outcomes of government activity. In the aftermath of Supreme Court decisions declaring much of the New Deal unconstitutional, the new Social Security legislation took its place as the centerpiece of the president's program. That legislation, decried by the Republicans, was probably the central policy issue of the 1936 election. The Democrats worried a great deal about Republican attacks on Social Security and looked for ways to answer these attacks. Noting the importance of New York to FDR's reelection and fearful that Al Smith's defection might hurt the president's prospects in November, for instance, Louise Lazell, director of the GNL's Speakers' Bureau, wrote to John C. Winant, a Republican and former governor of New Hampshire and the nation's first chair of the Social Security Board, asking for his support in the effort to "swing the state in the right direction for Governor Lehman and, of course, for the President." In a revealing postscript, she added, "Last night William Hard and McCarl gave one of the coldest-blooded analyses of our national financial situation—all dollars and cents—no human values. I think you are the one to answer in terms of human suffering, red-blooded and possibly red revolution, if relief is not carried through and social security not maintained in the future."[41] This postscript encapsulates much of the Roosevelt campaign's approach to the election: Republicans were cold-hearted financiers who understood little and cared less about the human suffering caused by the Depression. On the one hand this was wrong because it was selfish and neglected the entirety of the national community. On the other hand it was shortsighted, because if those who were suffering most did not have that suffering alleviated, revolution became possible. Roosevelt's reforms were thus offered as a humanistic and compassionate response to suffering, thus appealing to the Left, and as a moderate response to the perils of revolution, thus likely to appeal to centrists.

Moderate voices were important to the 1936 campaign, even in their relative absence. Many voters were concerned that the president had veered too far to one side or the other (one proof among many that he was indeed committed

54   VOTING DELIBERATIVELY

to the center) and wrote to the White House expressing their fears that he was courting the "radical vote" and neglecting the "thrifty middle class."[42] These fears were not being ameliorated by the parties. There was some hope that they could be addressed by a combination of ostensibly nonpartisan action and interpersonal networks. These networks, by offering education and discussion, also encouraged the more reasonable and deliberative side of mass politics, an especially important tendency in those cacophonous times. They encouraged citizens to see the national government as integral to their lives and to focus on the policy outcomes government produced as an evaluative measure of its performance. They also encouraged citizens to understand government in what FDR called "human terms" both in their lives and in the lives of others in their increasingly national community.

The Committee of One

The Great Depression challenged many American myths, but perhaps none took so heavy a beating as the myth of "rugged individualism," the idea that success was available if one only worked hard enough. Failure to achieve material success was thus attributable not to systemic inequalities but to individual inadequacies. The prevalence of this myth, so useful to supporting capitalism in general, proved debilitating to many as the economic structures crumbled.[43] The newly poor and those on the dole suffered the most, becoming listless, enervated, and docile.[44] The paternalism of New Deal programs seemed to be making matters worse and increased fears that government programs were eroding the work ethic and individualistic values on which the nation was based. Those fears were also widely shared within the administration and by the president.[45]

In a related vein, the New Deal also exacerbated fears that "affirmative government was destroying American freedom."[46] Freedom was thought to be endangered both by restricting the role of the private sphere and by replacing that sphere with governmental action. Just as individual citizens were likely to become passive recipients of governmental largesse, as the private sphere—the sphere of individual action—narrowed, the perceived ability of individuals to control their own destinies also shrank.

Roosevelt's extrapartisan organizations, such as the Committee of One, depended on individual action. They assumed that private individuals, acting on their own, were perfectly capable of understanding complex governmental policies and were able to explain them to others. These organizations thus encouraged a specific kind of citizenship. In a January 1936 radio address, Roosevelt had asked his listeners to constitute themselves as a "Committee of One," dedicated to learning the facts about the New Deal, American politics, and the campaign. "To that end," wrote the chair of the CO Executive Board, Senator Bennett Champ Clark (D-MO), "the Committee of One for the Re-election of President Roosevelt has been organized." His correspondents were asked not only if they wanted to be members but also, "Do you want to lend your aid to the fulfillment of the great human purposes of the Roosevelt Administration? Do you want to put your shoulder to the wheel in your community in order that the progress of these last three years may be continued?" They were assured that "THERE IS NO OBLIGATION; THERE ARE NO DUES" and exhorted, "DON'T SIGN unless you BELIEVE in the ideals of President Roosevelt and in his re-election."[47] Note in particular that the CO stressed only Roosevelt's ideals, not the actions of his administration or the platform of his political party. Party identification presupposes a more or less permanent affiliation. The CO asked for no such commitment, requiring no money and specifically promising no obligation. All that voters had to do was believe in particular ideals and work for FDR's reelection.

The CO, like the GNL, was ancillary to the Democratic Party. Indeed, party chair Jim Farley was active on behalf of the CO. He penned a "confidential" letter to Democrats, noting that "it is necessary that we obtain a wider representation in certain counties. That is why we are turning to you, as we know that in your own town and county you probably know names of loyal relatives and friends who will be glad to lend a hand in this worthy cause, persons whose hearts beat in sympathy with the great human purposes of President Roosevelt." The mechanism was dependent on individual personal contacts and networks working through a nationally directed organization. In this case, Farley announced that "we would like to have names outside of politics. It seems to me that especially desirable would be men who have something of a public contact, but not seeking office or reward. Women members we have found invariably to be reliable, trustworthy, and with a high sense of loyalty." The CO thus desired and created a particular kind of citizen, one who had a "public contact" and was a leader in civic affairs but who served without seeking office or expecting rewards. Its leaders were free of the taint of professional politics. The CO was set up an ancillary to but not in competition with the national party.[48]

So important was this aspect of the CO, in fact, that Farley wrote, "Please remember that these persons will in no way supplant the regular Democratic organization. They will merely afford this special Committee a means of getting a better distribution, through sympathetic sources, of campaign material and other pertinent data as the campaign develops."[49] Farley was not encouraging the development of organizations that would rival his own, and he was quick to assure leaders of local party organizations that he was not asking them to encourage rivals to their own power, either. Members of the CO would be neither aspiring to office nor hoping for patronage—the party organization was not to be threatened by this new extrapartisan one. The place of each was clearly demarcated, and Farley argued that party officials should support the extrapartisan organizations because to the extent that these temporary bodies were successful, party officials would be reaping the rewards.

Farley also approached members of Congress, supplying them with lists of "every postoffice [sic] in your congressional district where we do not have even a single member."[50] In this case, the implied stick was more obvious than the carrots being offered to local party officials. Post offices were one of the most direct forms of patronage Farley, as postmaster general, controlled. Members of Congress were being not-so-subtly reminded that there were post offices in their districts where office holders were not doing their part to support Roosevelt's reelection. Those members, who were all benefiting from Farley's largesse, were being reminded of their obligations to Farley and to the Roosevelt campaign. They were also being reminded that careful records were being kept. The implication was that further rewards would—or would not—be forthcoming based on the support documented in those records.

Such letters notwithstanding, the CO was even less of an organization, in traditional terms, than the GNL. Clark sent out a variety of pamphlets, for instance, with titles like *12 Long Weary Tragic Years* and *Questions and Answers: Business and Economic Catechism of the Roosevelt Administration*, along with a letter asking correspondents to "please read them so that you can explain the facts to others, and distribute the copies where you know they will do the most good."[51] There were no meetings and no dues. (There were pledge cards, which automobile owners could sign, promising to help transport voters to the polls on Election Day. In return for a pledge, they received a bumper sticker, campaign button, and a picture of the president labeled, "Re-Elect Roosevelt.")[52] The responsibilities of committee members were amorphous. It was perfectly possible to be affiliated with the CO based on nothing more than identification with Roosevelt and support for his reelection. It could also mean more than that. Committee members could, and ideally would, become tireless advocates for the New Deal and its president.

The CO was not a tightly defined organization, but members were not left without help or resources, either. Clark, for example, sent charter members letters providing them with "an outline of the various problems that will confront us in the campaign and ways for overcoming them." CO members were thus encouraged to think of themselves as part of the campaign and, as part of that campaign, were given help and support. They were treated as welcome members of a community. The campaign literature associated with the CO emphasized this sense of belonging and also reminded members that they were fighting both for a specific version of the American community and against another version. In one of his letters, for example, Clark asked members to note how many pictures of the president were on display in their communities and how well organized they considered the local campaign organization. "In other words, we are depending upon you to keep us informed as to the opposition as well as our own situation."[53] Members were thus encouraged to consider themselves as part of a larger whole, to conceive of citizenship and participation as one and the same.

The CO made it a point to reach out to independent voters. Clark wrote in August, for instance, a letter encouraging them to become charter members of the CO, "an organization working for the President's re-election outside of party circles." The letter, it appeared, was prompted by a conversation he had on a train, with a veteran who had voted for FDR in 1932 but was not planning on voting for his reelection. Clark, of course, "would not take this lying down, so knowing the true facts, I gave them to him straight from the shoulder, in a friendly way, to be sure. Pretty soon, he began to see he was wrong" and that "his mind had been poisoned by newspapers, gossip, rumors, and other insidious propaganda spread by thoughtless people and Republicans." The campaign, as depicted in this letter, was a contest between the forces who knew the "true facts" and the propaganda and malicious rumors spread by people who were "thoughtless" or who "wanted to get back in and would do anything to gain their ends."[54] By making the gulf between the sides stark and a matter of moral choice, such letters indicated how high the stakes of this election were and encouraged independents to vote for FDR. Because the CO existed "outside of party circles," independents did not have to form or to change existing party allegiances. They only had to listen to Clark's "message of true Americanism" and vote for the president. Citizenship, it appeared, could function independently of party. Perhaps true citizens even functioned best independently of political parties. The Democratic Party might reap the benefits of CO organizations, but any such consequences were secondary to the goal of the president's reelection.

The Committee of One was, at least in terms of numbers, remarkably successful, By October 1936 it had arranged for the production of 9.6 million fliers, 2.4 million pictures of Roosevelt, 1.5 million bumper stickers, 350,000 labels, 400,000 honor roll rosters, and 350,000 instruction sheets. These materials were collated into sets and mailed to some 350,000 recipients.[55] Reaching so many people, each of whom had theoretically pledged to personally advocate for the president's programs and his reelection, was, for the time, a noteworthy achievement. The CO was an interesting innovation in that it sought to combine what we normally think of as the prevailing model of retail politics—characterized by interpersonal connections—with the developing means of wholesale politics, reaching, through the mass media, an increasingly inchoate, mobile, and mass public. The CO used mass communication by mailing campaign kits in bulk and sought to take advantage of the new national mobility, including bumper stickers as part of their campaign kits, as well as capitalizing on the importance of more traditional interpersonal communication.

The effort also seems to have been successful in attracting interest—350,000 campaign kits were mailed in early October 1936; by the first of November Emil Hurja reported to Jim Farley that the CO had some 537,000 members and that 51,287,500 pieces of campaign literature had been distributed. The campaign had thus, according to Hurja, spent "between 8 and 10 cents apiece" for members (and likely Roosevelt voters), a price Hurja considered "damned cheap." Also important to Hurja was the fact that the CO campaign had resulted in 25,000 pledge cards, signers of which had been asked to communicate with their county chairs and who were likely to have been instrumental in the efforts to turn out the vote.[56]

Members of the Committee of One were given "Special Instructions" as part of their campaign kit. They were encouraged to "talk to voters," "wear the button," "go where the crowds go," "show the picture," "meet the women," and "get the voters out." The campaign considered two other matters "of vital importance": getting pledges from auto owners and completing the honor roll. The pledges, of course, were important in terms of voter turnout. The honor roll seemed to offer nothing more than "a permanent record of your accomplishments," but as a motivational tool may have been important—individuals would feel much better about submitting lengthy rolls to campaign headquarters.[57]

Motivation was clearly a goal. The special instructions, for instance, made careful note of the fact that the president himself "has expressed great interest, admiration, and thankfulness for the wonderful work you and others fellow members have been doing."[58] Members thus not only had Roosevelt's attention and gratitude, but they were also encouraged to think of themselves as part of a larger enterprise. They may have been only "one," but they were also part of a "committee"—individuals, in the best American tradition, but also members of a community. Members could thus be part of an enterprise that included rural and urban individuals representing different religions and regions, a powerfully inclusive element. But because all activity was local, those members never had to encounter those who were actually different from them in any significant way, and it was thus powerfully reassuring.

The contributions of individuals were specifically depicted as critical to the campaign's success, even its survival, enabling every member to feel important to the overall enterprise. According to the CO, "because our campaign funds are limited, and as we do not have the war chest and backing of the Rockefellers, Morgans, Duponts, Mellons, etc., we have had to limit the amount of material that we send you. However, by being very careful to distribute this only where you know it will do the most good, we are sure you will be able to make it go a long way."[59] The Roosevelt campaign was pitted not against the Republicans but against the combined interests of "the Rockefellers, Morgans, Duponts, Mellons, etc." It was a remarkably personalized campaign of the many against the privileged few. But, the instructions seemed to imply, the endeavor was not hopeless, because the many could rely on the good judgment of every individual member. Those members understood that resources were scarce and precious; they would display campaign material only where it would "do the most good." Roosevelt supporters were thus a certain kind of citizen, able to understand policy and to educate others, capable of exercising individual judgment, and mindful of the resources available to them. They identified with the "common man," but they had talents and abilities that the elite overlooked, discounted, even sneered at. Roosevelt, however, understood those abilities. He knew that these voters and potential voters were good national stewards, and Roosevelt, as their leader who encouraged these attitudes and behaviors, was therefore also a good steward for the nation. Voters were being encouraged not to think of it as a campaign waged between two parties but as a campaign fought out over issues understood in terms of individuals, with FDR on one side and people like "the Rockefellers" on the other.

This message was underlined in other campaign materials. One flyer, for example, bore the large headline, "What About the National Debt?" Below that headline, in an eye-catching box, the message continued, "A campaign of fear is being attempted to frighten voters to return to power the discredited gang that brought about the Hoover deflation. Thinking citizens will not be misled by these tactics. WHAT ARE THE FACTS?" The flyer contained both data on prices for various commodities and an argument based on those data. The presentation was easy to read, the argument clear—deflation as strongly associated with Hoover and the public's animosity toward the former president was used to taint Roosevelt's collective opposition. Voters were asked to "study these figures." The flyer admitted that the national debt was, as of 1936, a staggering $31 billion, a sum that would cost every farmer, assuming every citizen paid an equal cost of that debt, $242.80. But after noting that most of this debt had been inherited from the Hoover administration, the text indicated that compared to what it would have cost that same farmer to pay an equal share of the debt in 1932, factoring in the rise in farm prices since the beginning of the Roosevelt administration and "[measuring it] in terms of a farmers' real money—the things he produces—the national debt is less today than it was when the Roosevelt Administration took office."[60] The logic seems obscure, the math a little peculiar. But the message is clear: farmers understood the relationships between crop prices and the burden of debt they personally held relative to the overall national debt.

So on the one hand, we have the Roosevelt campaign, which made arguments based on data and thus is presumed to be making dispassionate, scientifically based decisions for the good of the nation. On the other hand, we have a "gang" of fear-mongering, power-seeking politicians, who are presumably distorting the truth to serve their own selfish ends. "Thinking citizens," defined here as Roosevelt supporters, would study the data and arrive at their own conclusions. Those voters could be trusted to do the right thing by him as he could be trusted to do the right thing by them. Voters were not condescended to. They were presumed to be able to follow logic, to do simple calculations, and to derive from both the content and the form of the campaign communication which candidate could best be trusted.

The flyer also attacked the logic of Roosevelt's opponents more directly, and again with reference to the candidate and his invidious backers rather than his party. "Governor Landon's supporters are telling farmers, home-owners, the independent business man, and, in fact, every citizen that the national debt must be paid in equal amounts by each person, irrespective of his wealth or earnings. Perhaps that is what Governor Landon would recommend if he were President. Perhaps the Landon supporters are remembering in the last year of the Hoover Administration, J. P. Morgan, the wealthy international banker, and his 32 rich partners paid no federal income tax."[61] Note the combination of prospective and retrospective voting appeals here. The past, in which the wealthy were privileged, would return in the future if Landon's supporters had their way. Landon here is depicted neither as actually proposing equal taxation, nor as supporting Morgan. Instead, it is his supporters who are out to recapture government and use it to their own selfish ends, who are the active participants. Landon is merely a tool in the hands of those who are waging a "campaign of misrepresentation." Landon almost disappears as a target, replaced by Morgan and his thirty-two rich friends.

Finally, above a cartoon of an elephant wearing a top hat and marching resolutely up the line on a graph depicting the nation's financial improvement while carrying a sign stating, "The country is going to the dogs," the flyer's final headline is "The Humanity of Debt." The text following that headline makes the case for FDR's reelection in blunt terms: "An enlightened Eastern newspaper, the Philadelphia Record, discussing the national debt had this to say: 'President Roosevelt had to decide between borrowing money and letting the country suffer as Hoover let it suffer. Roosevelt took the human view. Roosevelt took the view that money was the servant of man, not his master. Roosevelt took the view that there is no greater, wiser investment in the stability of the United States of American and the welfare of the people.'"[62] This text is consistent with the other campaign material and underlines the arguments made by the Roosevelt campaign throughout the 1936 election: compassion for the people in the form of relief was both the right thing to do from a strictly human point of view and was also the policy most likely to promote national stability. Roosevelt's opponents, shortsightedly interested only in their own material well-being, disregarded both the demands of a suffering people and the requirements of national stability. The campaign material assumed that voters could make connections between abstract ideas (the deficit and national stability) and between those ideas and the candidate. Note, though, that the Republicans are the missing element here. Hoover (the past) is mentioned, but Landon (and any possible future) is absent. This campaign is all about FDR.

Given the ways in which data are mined today for all kinds of purposes, it is interesting that the White House seemed reluctant to make much use of the vast amount of information it compiled. While Hurja, with his passion for data, collected membership by state, tracked growth over time, and noted the professions of members (categorized as farmers, physicians, and others), there seems to have been no effort made at tracking committee members or their activities. There appears to have been only minimal effort at using the committee as a fund-raising mechanism.[63] Such developments would become increasingly important elements in national campaigns. They began in efforts like these, which entailed efforts at organizing and mobilizing independent voters as well as partisans toward the reelection of a particular candidate. There were virtually no efforts made at turning membership in the GNL or in the CO into membership in the Democratic Party. The point was not party building. All efforts were extended toward building support for the candidate.

The CO's goal was primarily to encourage individual action, not action organized by party. In this sense, the CO advocated a particular kind of citizenship, one that sought to mobilize the prevailing faith in "rugged individualism" in the interests of a communitarian spirit. That is, the CO relied on individual expertise and action to foster collective action. The assumption was that any individual, regardless of social status or educational background, could understand the intricacies of governmental policy, no matter how apparently complicated those policies were. More than that, these individuals, even the most poorly educated among them, could serve as educators for their communities. This was consistent with what Adam Cohen has called Roosevelt's effort to displace an ethic of rugged individualism with one centered on community responsibility.[64]

It is interesting that this effort would occur outside of the boundaries set by the political parties. Roosevelt was a strong partisan and supported the Democratic Party in many important ways. But he was also fully capable of going outside of the party to secure what he considered to be important ideological ends, ends consistent with party philosophy. He was happy to work within the Democratic Party, but as his behavior in the purge indicated, he was not willing to understand party goals as more important that his own. Roosevelt thus had a great deal to do with the creation of extrapartisan means of organizing the electorate, means that contributed to the rise of candidate-centered politics. Those means were, as we have seen, on display throughout the 1936 election.

Conclusion

The 1936 election was organized around, and had as its main issue, the person and politics of Franklin D. Roosevelt.[65] Perhaps no story typifies the effect Roosevelt's form of personalized politics has better than this one, which appears in a biography of Frances Perkins, his secretary of labor. Following Roosevelt's funeral, "Frances found herself beside a soldier, who spoke to her without looking in her direction. 'I felt as if I knew him,' he said. 'Yes,'" Frances said. The young man paused. 'I felt as if he knew me, and I felt as if he liked me.'"[66] This feeling is difficult to explain, given that the soldier, like the millions of Americans who felt similarly connected to Roosevelt, never met him. Because of that sense of intimacy, and the personal loyalty it engendered, citizens were also loyal to the New Deal. This loyalty was transferred in turn to the Democratic Party. But as Milkis notes, this constituted a reversal of previous realignments, in which loyalty to party preceded and dominated loyalty to the individual president. The New Deal coalition inculcated partisanship on a level that would dominate American politics into the 1960s. But even as he created one of the most dominant electoral coalitions in political history, Roosevelt also encouraged forms of extrapartisan organization that facilitated the rise of candidate-centered politics. These extrapartisan organizations encouraged inclusiveness, debate, and the enactment of a certain kind of citizenship that depended on the person of the president.

Certainly, there had been personalized campaigns before; the 1840 campaign featuring "Tippecanoe and Tyler too" comes most readily to mind. But that campaign, also notable for its use of music and log cabin imagery, was markedly different from this one. It did not, for example, offer its standard-bearer as a lens through which issues could be understood. It did not, in fact, really focus on issues at all. Harrison's war record substituted for issues and served as a distraction from them. In 1936, however, the issues and the candidate were conflated. Roosevelt served as a condensation symbol for the issues, and citizens were encouraged to see their interests and his election as the same.

Under Roosevelt, the Democratic National Party presided over a collection of short-lived ad hoc organizations that in many ways indicated the shape of politics to come. They served as a means of reconciling various interests that otherwise might have been understood as endangering national unity, and they did so by encouraging a certain kind of citizenship appropriate for a mass democracy. Roosevelt critic and New Deal analyst Amity Shlaes sees in this a shift from republican to democratic modes of governance.[67] It was certainly a time in which presidents became unmoored from strong allegiances to party and developed a personal politics, fueled by the president, the media, and the forces of reform that enabled them to enjoy ascendancy over the parties in the public sphere.

The press seemed to have much less much influence in the 1936 election than it had previously wielded.[68] Roosevelt, frustrated with the press, sought other ways of getting his version of his administration—and his sense of his opposition—out to the public. Ad hoc extrapartisan organizations such as the Good Neighbor League and the Committee of One served the Roosevelt campaign not least because they provided individuals with trusted and reliable means of cutting through the media noise and controversy to understand facts and arguments. Even as the mass media burgeoned during these years, it also appeared to be less credible than the arguments of community leaders. And it was those leaders the Roosevelt campaign sought to capture with the GNL and the CO. They represented the settled aspect of local community, a part of American life that many citizens considered under siege by the economic dislocations and social changes of the early twentieth century. If the local was going to be lost to the national, the fabric of social community was also endangered. New means of building that community had to be found.

While Shlaes disagrees, others contend that this was a time in which a new sense of social obligation replaced the emphasis on individual achievement and "rugged individualism."[69] This new citizenship, as Roosevelt advocated for it, encouraged the crossing of political boundaries set by race, religion, and geography. Roosevelt proposed a community based on values that transcended these demarcations of difference and encouraged citizens to become members of that community.[70] Where the parties had once served—and in many ways continued to serve—as mechanisms for organizing the electorate, it was now increasingly possible for other, more temporary, and ad hoc organizations to enable citizens to come to a shared understanding of themselves and their political world. Under Roosevelt, and through such vehicles as the Good Neighbor League and the Committee of One, candidates, rather than their parties, came to be the dominant symbol through which Americans understood their politics.

The Roosevelt campaign thus exemplifies several important trends: candidate-centered campaigns, a belief in the national government as responsible for the well-being and security of its citizens, and a related belief that citizens should look to that government for that security and well-being. Importantly, FDR sought to encourage deliberation as well as participation. The campaign encouraged citizens to believe in their own capacities as citizens, to educate themselves and those around them, and to participate in elections. Parties endured and continued to matter, as they endure and continue to matter today. But candidates and their organizations galvanize the public in ways that parties are less able to do. Even as Roosevelt sought to use party, he developed mechanisms that undermined the parties. One such mechanism was extrapartisan campaign organizations. Another was the increasing tendency, also apparent in the 1936 election, of understanding citizens not as members of political parties but as members of clearly defined interest groups.

3

MOBILIZING THE VOTE, CONTAINING THE PUBLIC

Interest groups and the identities on which they depend predated the New Deal, having their origins in charitable organizations both in Europe and in the United States. In the American context, the power and longevity of such groups was illustrated by the growth and development of the Abolition Movement. As powerful as those groups were in gaining specific policies such as abolition and suffrage, individuals were not constituted politically primarily as members of those groups. They were understood as advocates of policy, not as members of largely ascriptive groups. In the 1930s, that changed. As members of the mass public were increasingly understood through their affiliation with interest groups, campaigns and the governments that resulted from them organized the electorate along group lines and understood the public's policy preferences in terms of the interests associated with those groups. This paradoxically gave (some) citizens access to government while also narrowing their ability to articulate a range of preferences. For members of some groups, of course, access to government and its largesse was sharply restricted. Understanding the public in terms of group affiliation, then, both opened the government to a wide and diverse electorate and helped the government contain and manage it.

This understanding of politics stemmed from an effort—openly and frequently articulated by the president—to find ways of including more people in the processes of governmental decision making and to allow the president to advocate for the many against the interests of the few. This is what Iris Marion

Young refers to as self-development and self-determination, two criteria for what she considers inclusive democracy.[1] But government could easily become overwhelmed by the demands created by this new inclusiveness unless it could somehow be managed. The focus on group membership and identity was one method of controlling new pressures on government and its leaders.

The Roosevelt White House became one of the first to constitute the electorate as what are now understood as interest groups.[2] Not only did members of labor unions, women, African Americans, Jews, and Catholics flock to the New Deal banner, but during the 1930s these groups came to understand these affiliations as politically relevant and politically central in ways they previously that had not. They competed and cooperated with one another over policy, and they organized themselves to do so more effectively. So powerful were they, in fact, that by 1937 polling advocates were touting the public-opinion poll as the only mechanism able to contend with such groups' ability to define and mobilize public opinion.[3] Party leaders were still the most reliable means of projecting and turning out the vote, but they continually lost ground in this aspect of campaigning to groups who were organized by interest rather than by ward and who expected to be rewarded with policy rather than patronage. As one analyst put it, "As the New Deal advanced, it moved away from 'national' solutions toward 'group' solutions and to a definition of citizenship that included identification with a social group. Such democratic group self-government could satisfy individuals' desire for self-expression and control of their lives and might also develop the habits and virtues of democracy in the mass of the people."[4] Group identification, then, became more than a way of organizing and mobilizing the electorate. Those activities, in turn, contributed to the development of a new kind of citizen who stood in a new sort of relationship with the national government. Rather than deploring group membership and activity as inimical to democracy, the Roosevelt administration in general and his 1936 campaign in particular fostered such membership and such activity as a means of organizing and mobilizing the electorate and also as a method of encouraging a particular kind of citizen, suited to the developing political economy of the twentieth century.

In this chapter I examine three such groups, which represent the range of ways of which group affiliation was managed in the 1936 election. First, I look at Mary W. (Molly) Dewson, vice-chair of the Democratic National Committee and head of its Women's Division. The mobilization tactics she pioneered illustrate the ways in which the Roosevelt campaign sought to include (some) previously overlooked constituents and indicate some of the ways in which political hierarchies were both reinforced and altered during the New Deal as new constituencies were incorporated into existing political structures.[5] Second, I look at organized labor, for in 1936 organized labor had a much more important role than it had previously enjoyed. Labor also had a DNC division to call its own, but labor was less dependent on that relationship than were either women or African Americans. Newly authorized and empowered by the National Industrial Recovery Act and the Wagner Act, labor unions worked within the Democratic Party structure but in 1936 also displayed considerable independence from that structure. As unions became more powerful and more accepted as legitimate aspects of American political life, union organizations would come to be central to Democratic campaigns, but they continued to operate as independent entities.

Finally, I treat the case of African Americans, who, like women and labor, had a division of the DNC dedicated to their recruitment and mobilization. Unlike women, African Americans had no advocate like Molly Dewson, close to the Roosevelts both personally and politically and able to press for their organizational interests.[6] Unlike labor, they had only a small organizational base outside of the party structure that concentrated on organizing the vote and pushing for policy. In the North, African Americans were increasingly active politically and increasingly organized as well. But even as African Americans became a core constituency of the New Deal coalition, they remained marginal to it in many ways, and the Democrats as a national party maintained considerable national power based directly on black disenfranchisement. Despite their willingness to recruit and mobilize African Americans in the North and West, Roosevelt and the Democratic Party he led continued black oppression as a foundation of their national coalition.

This chapter thus indicates the ways in which Roosevelt worked with the Democratic Party to locate important sources of support, to organize those constituents as members of politically empowered groups, and to use that group membership as a means of mobilizing the vote and pressuring the government. Group membership came to rival partisan affiliation as means of linking citizens to the government and to the president, who increasingly came to symbolize and direct that government. Reading citizenship through group affiliation made government more accessible to at least some of its citizens and provided a mechanism through which the increasingly complicated mass electorate could be contained and made available to government.

The Women's Division

Many of the women active in the New Deal got their political start as members of suffrage organizations. Others came to politics through the vehicle of social work, in the 1920s and 1930s still a developing profession and one of the few open to educated women.[7] Women played more important roles in the New Deal than they are often given credit for, as only Eleanor Roosevelt and Frances Perkins are generally recognized. Women's roles were conditioned by the culture in which they were embedded—reflecting both the continued importance of racialized and maternalist understandings of women and the potential for women's empowerment brought about by Progressive reformers and institutionalized in the Nineteenth Amendment.[8] So while women increasingly worked, it was also widely argued throughout the 1930s that married women should be allowed to work only if their husbands remained unemployed.[9] During the Depression, women lost their jobs at a faster rate than men, providing one more example, were it needed, that women's work was seen as ancillary to that of men. Women, empowered on the one hand, were caught in a double bind created by that empowerment on the other.

One of the great myths of women's history is that between suffrage and the 1960s there was little to be said about women's activism.[10] Even Howard Zinn argues that the great contribution women made during the 1930s was in labor legislation, not in advancing their own interests.[11] Many of the women who worked for suffrage continued working in politics, both on what they considered "women's issues," like the Equal Rights Amendment, and on other issues such as the minimum wage and child labor. The New Deal itself offered enormous opportunities for women and employed numerous women in public roles—in such numbers in fact, that the record would not be matched until the 1960s.[12] Molly Dewson was one such woman. Born in Boston and educated at Wellesley, Dewson worked with a variety of social-welfare organizations in Massachusetts and New York, meeting the Roosevelts, and becoming very close to both of them.[13] Like many of the women of her time, she was deeply embedded in a network of active women. She was equally comfortable in the male-dominated world of partisan politics.[14]

After years of working for social causes, Dewson worked for FDR's reelection as governor of New York and in his first presidential campaign. During the first term, she served as vice-chair of the Democratic National Campaign Committee and also headed up the Women's Division of the Democratic National

Committee (DNC). She resigned from her formal leadership role early in the first term, but remained as chair of the Women's Division Advisory Committee (an entity that did not actually formally exist), a position that allowed her influence in party councils and with the president while also permitting her to maintain her health and protect her personal relationship with Polly Porter.[15] She exercised considerable power and influence within the DNC in general and at the 1936 convention in particular.[16] She worked hard to garner the women's vote for FDR in 1936 by actively recruiting women to the Democratic Party, and then organizing them as important contributors to the campaign.[17] As a result of her efforts, women were active in party matters and also earned jobs in the administration.[18] Her goal was the full integration of women into the party apparatus. That goal was never fully achieved, but while Dewson remained politically active, great strides were made in finding ways to include women in the Democratic Party on all levels.[19] Her work as head of the Women's Division, a role she used to argue for that integration, is one example of the ways she worked within the system to both reinscribe women's difference and argue for women's incorporation. In the process, Dewson became one of the most powerful women in the Democratic Party, and she exemplifies the kind of organization along group lines that helped Roosevelt win in 1936.

In her role as head of the Women's Division, Dewson did a great deal of organizing among female party leaders, and she did so with the zeal of a true believer. In one memo, for instance, she noted, "The Jackson Day dinners opened the 1936 campaign. It will be a long, hotly debated fight between the vested interests and those concerned for the welfare of the average man. Our great task is to prevent any Democrat from being stampeded by the Republican dust storm and to convince enough independents they want Roosevelt reelected to win in November 1936."[20] Despite the rather badly mixed metaphors, it is clear here that she understood her job in much the same way as we currently understand campaigns: the task was to motivate party members and to persuade the uncommitted. What makes Dewson so interesting, however, isn't her understanding of these fairly obvious premises, but the imagination she brought to these tasks and the ways in which she incorporated women into what had been an exclusively male domain.

As with many of the women of her generation, a number of her organizational ideas derived from her experiences with the fight for women's suffrage, experiences that gave her both managerial expertise and a network of women from whom she could draw support. She worked and acted at an important intersection of women's politics. She argued that women were fundamentally different from men and should be allowed to bring those differences in the service of progressive politics. She often advocated legislation that protected women as a special class. She also argued, however, that women were as interested in—and as capable of understanding—national issues as men. Her persuasive campaigns were organized around both of these beliefs and indicate the ways in which gender was negotiated throughout the 1936 election and the New Deal.

For example, she outlined suggestions for Democratic campaign activities, including ways to increase enthusiasm (speakers and programs); fund-raise (bingo parties and donkey banks); encourage voter registration and turnout; and appeal to independent voters (newspaper ads, press releases, radio broadcasts, open meetings, speakers, and outreach to civic organizations). In every aspect of the campaign, she stressed the role and importance of the Women's Division, which she organized with an eye to both the national campaign and a keen recognition of the value of local control.[21] The prime goal was to "Get Inside That Door!"—a goal that reflected her faith, and that of the Roosevelt campaign, in the retail politics of personal relationships.[22]

Dewson "organized the 'reporter plan,' under which women in every locality were charged with responsibility of learning and telling about government activities."[23] She mobilized local women, educated by the campaign to understand national issues, to encourage the vote in their own neighborhoods. In so doing, she made sure those women had organizational support and an awareness of how they fit into the bigger state and national picture.[24] "No woman," Dewson said, "is too busy, too tired, or too dumb to help."[25] Dewson's Reporter Plan, indeed, all her campaign strategies, were based in that premise.[26]

She articulated the ABCs of campaigning (A is for autos getting voters to the polls; B is for ballots marked for FDR; C is for calling to remind voters to vote), and she focused on the importance of training, motivation, and the value of personal connections in accomplishing those goals.[27] She organized a series of precinct training schools for Democratic women and marketed them as a combination of the political ("get together to plan an overwhelming victory on November 5th"), the personal ("Bring your lunch! Meet your Democratic friends!"), and the organizational ("Demonstrations of streamlined ways to canvass the precinct, contact voters, convince first voters and independent voters, get voters to the polls").[28] Dewson thus made participation socially satisfying as well as politically useful. Women were encouraged to see themselves as empowered through their personal connections and as connected to a vast web of equally empowered women across the nation. Their gender—and the social and cultural practices surrounding it—were construed as political assets rather than as liabilities that had to be overcome.

Politics was treated by Dewson and the Women's Division as a communal enterprise. Women were consistently assured that they had the backing and support of the national party. Dewson sent a steady stream of material aimed at helping women structure their own local organizations. Among her other accomplishments were the creation of the Rainbow Fliers. She also provided sample questions and answers for Interrogation Teas and *Farming Answers for the Heckler in the Back of the Room*.[29] The Rainbow Fliers covered fourteen different policy areas, each bearing its own color. Assembled, they evoked a rainbow, and they visually and textually underlined the breadth of New Deal programs.[30] The fliers included *Keeping Children Fed, Families Together*; *Men at Work*; *Farmers and Foreign Trade*; *Our Wealth of Earth and Water*; and *The Truth About Taxes*.[31] These issues were pitched to what could be understood as a "woman's perspective," but were not restricted to "women's issues." The policies under discussion were those considered important to the Roosevelt agenda. The fliers treated women as if they could grasp the complexities of tax policy and the effects of those policies on the family mortgage and as if they could both understand and have a stake in foreign-trade policy.[32] In her autobiography, Dewson wrote, "women had too long been adjuncts to men and we usually organized as auxiliaries or independently in women's clubs. Organizations of war veterans, I suppose, need auxiliaries to prepare dinner and to run social affairs, but where women's interest is equal to man's interest as in political parties, trade unions, and the Grange, there is no sense in separation."[33] You can practically hear the contempt dripping from her pen as she pities the poor veterans who are unable to arrange their own teas. The thought that women should be relegated to such roles in politics, the world of work, or advocacy was an abomination to her.

Dewson was not entirely free of the gender norms prevailing in the 1930s, however. The fliers were adapted into sandwich boards, suitable for wearing by "sandwich girls." She noted "twelve good-looking girls are needed to make a team. We are going to call them 'gloom chasers.'"[34] The use of pretty girls was one concession made to the tenor of the times in which she lived and also reflected her astute understand of mass marketing, even as such tactics reinforced the gender hierarchies she worked within. There were also inherent class biases (Interrogation Teas, for instance, evoke particular understandings of women as a political audience) and racial ones as well.[35] But mostly, she treated women as autonomous, reasoning, and important political actors and organizers rather than as spectacle or props in a male enterprise.

She designed pamphlets for "Mrs. County Leader" (note the implication that county leaders would be married), which warned, again with the mixed metaphors that were something of a trademark in her writing, "If you are inactive or flying around in circles, your county will be the stone that lets the arch collapse."[36] The pamphlet notes, "The voters live in all precincts; being just one woman, you can't talk with them all yourself; you must expand yourself." Herein lay the genius of her political organization. It was based on an intricate and expansive network of personal connections. She encouraged county leaders to "galvanize precinct leaders" through regular contact and specific direction. She noted that "if you are no spellbinder" one would be supplied by the state vice-chair.[37] The object was to register and mobilize women voters, and the way to do this, she argued, was through personal connections. County leaders met with precinct leaders who met with the women in their districts. These women were responsible for registering other women and making sure they reached the voting booth. They were armed with resources and with information about every conceivable policy. They were given what we would now call talking points as well as a range of tactical options (radio parties, donkey banks, rainbow fliers). The donkey banks were an especially important innovation. Individual banks, shaped like the Democratic donkey, were given to local women who solicited small donations. Once the banks were full of small change, local organizations held "donkey round-ups," during which the banks were opened and the change counted. The women were able to see that their small efforts amounted to a fairly large outcome, and all the money thus raised stayed in the local communities where it was raised, supporting various election efforts.

As the activities surrounding the donkey banks illustrate, through the work of the Women's Division individual women were encouraged to understand themselves as responsible and contributing members of the campaign. Other commitments, however, were also recognized: "Your county is your responsibility and there are no alibis. If John has lost his job or Mary has the measles, or you have broken your leg, you can resign and the sooner the better, but if you are the active county leaders, it's up to you to act active. If *Mr.* County Leader is inactive and wants you to be a figurehead, don't listen to him, for this book, dedicated to you, tells you what to do to WIN VOTES."[38] Here, the primacy of familial obligations was underlined—women who participated in FDR's campaign were not expected to subordinate their domestic concerns to that campaign. In case of conflict, women were encouraged to put their families first. But if they remained in the campaign they were not necessarily subordinate to men. They were not obliged to follow Mr. County Leader's lead. This gender heresy empowered women to see themselves as important actors in their own right. They rightfully had responsibilities to their families, and those responsibilities were taken seriously. But they were not to be allowed to interfere with the all-important task of reelecting Franklin D. Roosevelt.[39]

Through such prompts, women were encouraged to think of themselves as part of a greater enterprise. Dewson's pamphlet announced, "If you carry your county, Hooray! Or if you reduce the liability that your Republican county is to the Democratic counties in your state, twice Hooray!"[40] Women were not allowed to fail—activity in the Democratic cause mattered more than actual results. Victory was appreciated, of course, but even eroding the Republican margin came to be seen as a victory—even twice the victory of actually carrying a county. No county leader was allowed to think of her task as hopeless. Every small achievement contributed to the greater goal of a Roosevelt victory, and even small accomplishments became understood as major contributions to the wider enterprise.

While Dewson worked within and for the Democratic Party even in those efforts, women didn't have to be part of the formal Democratic Party organization to be important. Dewson mobilized individual women through programs like the Reporter Plan, an eight-week series of radio programs in which women learned about specific issues and were encouraged to talk, one-on-one, with other women, who were then encouraged to do the same. Publicity chairs were encouraged to work closely with the leaders of the plans to maximize their effectiveness.[41] The project included discussions, specifically from a "woman's perspective," on the Agricultural Adjustment Act, unemployment, the Works Progress Administration, credit agencies and homeownership, and taxation.[42] This is especially interesting because it's not limited to what we think of as women's issues but included subjects of concern to women as citizens while allowing for a particularized perspective on women. Here, too, women were understood as apprehending and acting on issues across the political spectrum, not merely those of narrowly understood domestic concerns. The Women's Division communicated to women in broad and inclusive terms and treated them as fully functioning members of the electorate. Women, for Dewson, were citizens, not merely "women citizens."

While Dewson and the Women's Division were, after 1933, formally part of the Democratic National Committee (prior to that it had been part of the Democratic National Campaign Committee, a structure that recognized Roosevelt's ambivalence concerning the party in 1932), the division was also relatively autonomous and operated outside of the formal party structure.[43] Even when working within the party, Roosevelt was also looking for ways to increase his leverage over it and was often using organizational techniques that reached out to individual voters and individuals understood through their group affiliations to do so. Just as he was happy to work outside bureaucratic structures to accomplish his programmatic ends, establishing a series of more or less formal working groups, agencies, committees and commissions, he was also demonstrably willing to operate outside of established party structures to accomplish his political ends.

So it is unsurprising that Dewson emphasized capturing the Republican and the uncommitted vote as well as that of Democratic women. She summed up her efforts in 1936 by stating, "Women had concentrated on the pivotal states and on reminding their silent voters, fact by fact, in easy words and by accurate figures that spoke for themselves, what Roosevelt had meant to them, their families, and their neighbors. We had made the silent voters aware of what they already knew, although somewhat vaguely, and gave them confidence in their opinions. We had not shot words into the air to fall to earth we knew not where, but had delivered them by hand in visible form to be pored over more than once because they were readable."[44] The Women's Division knew their audience, accommodated it, and courted it. Division members went door-to-door, they spoke to their friends and acquaintances, and they used every means possible to reach "silent voters." Dewson exhorted correspondents to ask their local radio stations to "put on a series of five talks that will interest the women."[45] These talks covered "Social Security," "A Future for the Farm Family," "A Home with Hope," "Belief in Relief," and "Recovery—It's Price and Premium." She noted that all speakers had two goals: the conversion of non-Democratic voters to the Roosevelt camp and the motivation of Democrats.[46]

This example is only one instance of her eagerness to use technology in the service of the Roosevelt campaign. In the summer of 1936, for example, she argued, "Campaigns are now conducted over the air," telling each "Radio Chairman" that "the essential thing is to have those listen in who have not decided on their choice for President."[47] She encouraged Democratic county leaders to host "Radio Parties," again focused on uncommitted voters and those whom we now refer to as "persuadables."[48] Even as early as 1936, Dewson was noting—and using—new technologies in an effort to reach uncommitted voters and was supplementing those technologies with traditional media such as postcards, fliers, sandwich boards, and newspaper ads.

Long before scholars and pundits were interested in the potential and problems of negative campaigning, Dewson understood the importance of countering attacks. She began a letter to "speakers," in the fall of 1936, for example, asserting, "The vicious propaganda regarding the Social Security Act now being circulated by the Republican party Administration, [sic] must be met."[49] She argued that the positive case for FDR and the Democrats had to be made consistently and forcefully, and with an eye toward both the local and the national. Dewson claimed that a good campaign involved both offense and defense, and she unhesitatingly organized the Women's Division in ways that allowed them to play both. Women were not confined to the genteel arena of politics. Dewson wanted then fully engaged in all aspects of campaigning and governing.

She modeled this engagement as well as preaching it. She spoke out personally in defense of Roosevelt, arguing in one radio address that "fear of poverty is NOT limited to the man of the house merely because he has the family to support and has to have a job. Concern for the neighbor's poverty is NOT limited to the woman of the house merely because she has more time to do personal welfare work. Destitution is sexless. So is kindness. No measure in President Roosevelt's program helps humanity so widely and so wisely" as Social Security.[50] Again, note that she does not segment politics into "issues" and "women's issues" but argued always that all issues crossed gender lines. She even tacitly argued here against the stereotypes implicit in those lines. Women were understood by Dewson, if not by the campaign and the administration as a whole, to be fully capable of understanding and acting in the political realm.

Thus, not only did Dewson contribute to the 1936 campaign and to the ways in which campaigns were (and are) conducted, but she also serves as both an example and exception to ways in which women and other minorities were treated under the New Deal. She had, for instance, a strong commitment to incorporating women in government at all levels, and she spent considerable time on patronage.[51] One author notes, "Symbolically at least, the New Deal marked a breakthrough in the role of women in public life. Roosevelt appointed the first female member of the cabinet in the nation's history, Secretary of Labor Frances Perkins. He also named more than 100 other women to positions at lower levels of the federal bureaucracy. But New Deal support for women operated within limits. Even many of the women in the administration were concerned not so much about achieving gender equality as about obtaining special protections for women."[52] Dewson's example indicates both the growing power of women under the New Deal and the limits on that power, for there were strong cultural and legal biases against the employment of women, which were strengthened by the fact of economic crisis.[53] These biases worked to keep women domesticated even as women like Dewson argued for and enacted a different kind of political potential.

But Dewson also indicates the ways in which the Roosevelt camp innovated in 1936. Democrats not only had a Women's Division but imbued it with autonomy and power. They understood women as a powerful constituency and actively worked to organize that constituency.[54] The Women's Division was fully integrated into the national party organization and worked on the local level toward national goals. Under the leadership of Molly Dewson, women were understood as intelligent, reasoning, and capable citizens, and their efforts were placed within a context of both domestic responsibility and personal empowerment. They were supplied with tools for success and support in learning to use those tools. The emphasis was on local organization to national ends, the most important of which was the reelection of Franklin D. Roosevelt.

Women, organized and mobilized along the ascriptive lines of gender, were encouraged to think of themselves as women and as citizens, not narrowly as women citizens whose interests were properly confined to "women's issues." The Women's Division accepted some gendered restrictions on women, recognizing, for instance, the primacy of domestic concerns. It undermined or violated others, insisting that women were as interested in and able to understand all government policy as much as men. Women, then, were both contained and mobilized as a group and were not likely, on the basis of the campaign, to think of group membership as a means of exerting governmental pressure. The Roosevelt administration spent considerably more time and energy on organized labor.

Labor

It is impossible to overestimate either the importance of labor in the 1930s or the level and extent of its dissatisfaction.[55] Industrial wage earners were particularly hard hit by the Depression. FDR is often credited with increasing the importance and autonomy of labor in American politics, an attribution not without irony, for he "was no instinctive friend" of unions.[56] Roosevelt had a sort of distant sympathy for labor, and especially with its aims, but he was a long way from seeing himself as a promoter of industrial unionism and, the promotion of unions had no place in his understanding of national economic policy.[57] The surge in labor-related violence in 1934–35 did little to make the president more comfortable, either. His secretary of labor, Frances Perkins, was equally ambivalent about labor and especially its leaders.[58]

During the first term, FDR found an advocate, if not a friend, in labor leader John L. Lewis. Labor was an integral part of his 1936 reelection campaign, and wage workers expected to be rewarded for that participation. When Roosevelt's second term became more about his fight with the Court and his internal battle with the Democratic Party exemplified in the "purge," labor became increasingly disaffected. Roosevelt irrevocably broke with Lewis in 1940; by then, however, labor was committed to the Democratic Party and to the president who led it.[59] In 1936, however, the extent of that allegiance was not yet clear.

As the New Deal increasingly separated labor from capital, political sides seemed to be drawn more and more starkly along class lines. Working people, angered by the continued Depression and the apparent unwillingness of the wealthy to make concessions, became increasingly organized and willing to use that organization to force concessions. Labor unrest intensified from 1934 on, and labor was, in conservative and even moderate circles, accused of fomenting Marxism, if not outright class war.[60]

That unrest convinced many liberals that domestic peace—and thus economic recovery—required a national labor law, one that guaranteed representation by unions to workers.[61] Probably nothing made more of a difference to labor than the passage of the Wagner Act in 1935.[62] The Wagner Act not only provided for the right to organize but threw the power of the federal government behind the protection of that right. Defending the act, Robert Wagner addressed fears that it would lead to a "labor dictatorship" and argued that it did not actually "encourage labor unionism." The act's supporters argued that labor was not given preferential treatment by this legislation but that it served only to "make the worker a free man [sic] in the economic as well as the political field."[63] The idea that workers had the right to both political and economic autonomy was a powerful one. It helps explain the allegiance such workers developed and maintained to both the New Deal and Roosevelt himself, whom they credited with advocating this idea.

But not all of labor's contributions were equally welcome. Ira Katznelson, for example, argues, "Above all, it was a cluster of issues concerning labor markets and labor unions that began to divide the Democratic Party more decisively."[64] At least partly, although Katznelson does not make this part of his argument, this division was due to the conflicts between "old stock," often skilled labor, and the newer immigrants, often working in less skilled fields.[65] Race provided its own set of difficulties as well.[66] Unions, especially the large, confederated unions, became places where these differences could be submerged in a developing sense of labor as a unified class.[67] Labor's unity was something of a double-edged sword, however, for as labor became stronger, it seemed to threaten established political as well as economic verities. The CIO made efforts to organize in the South and among African Americans, thus posing a threat to both the class and the racial hierarchies on which the structures of American politics depended.[68] Labor thus threatened social disorder on a variety of fronts, and the administration accommodated workers such that they could be disciplined into a political force supportive of the president and national stability. Unions functioned as a means of assimilating newer immigrants into the nation, and New Deal policies facilitated the assimilation of labor as a class into national politics. Containing and ordering labor was as important to Roosevelt as mobilizing it.

Newly empowered, then, and also indebted to the Roosevelt administration, labor had an important role in the 1936 election and represented one of the more contested of the interest-group arenas.[69] In one of the most controversial moves of the campaign, some employers put notes in pay packets condemning Social Security and claiming that the workers would have money deducted from their pay that they would never get back, as the program could not pay for itself.[70] Within days, the Democrats, largely because of the organizational skill behind the Women's Division, had replied and were issuing their own notices, fliers, and pamphlets, with titles such as *Don't Believe the Labor Spy in Your Pay Envelope* and *The Truth About Social Security*. These fliers encouraged workers to want security and to find it in the New Deal, which was associated with independence in old age, the promise of relief when unemployed, pensions for "needy people," and "care for helpless children."[71] Such tactics bolstered the image fostered by section 7(a) of the National Industrial Recovery Act and the Wagner Act that the New Deal and its president were committed to support for working people.[72] Labor never forgot its allegiance and became a mainstay of the Democratic coalition.

Despite this allegiance, union members in 1936 remained independent of the national party, who needed them every bit as much as labor needed friendly politicians. While the 1936 campaign maintained a "Labor Division," it was small, and relatively few of its documents remain in the Roosevelt Library—a fact that indicates the independence of labor as nothing else can, given the wealth of material available on, say, the Women's Division.

Social Security was a central issue in the campaign, and the White House took steps to counter Republican attacks on it, sending a variety of surrogates out on the campaign trail in defense of Social Security.[73] These attacks included arguments about the nature and extent of the taxes used to support Social Security, its tendency toward "socialized medicine," and its potential to redistribute wealth.[74] The Democrats even designed a forty-page pamphlet, *Economic Security in the Sunset of Life*, for use in the campaign.[75] The pamphlet contains personal testimony; statistical information; a portrait of the First Lady captioned, "America's Leading Social Worker"; and a plethora of evidence in support of Social Security. As with other forms of Roosevelt's campaign communication, the pamphlet treated voters as reasoning and capable of understanding complex policy. It also understood them as members of particular groups, all of which were united by their need for security, their belief that it was at least in part the government's obligation to provide for that security, and their faith that Franklin Roosevelt was committed to fulfilling that need and shared that belief. Given this treatment, especially when compared to the ways labor was understood by the Republicans, the loyalty of workers to the New Deal and the Democrats seems all but inevitable. The loyalty of African Americans, on the other hand, is a bit harder to explain.

African Americans and the Democratic Party

Prior to Roosevelt, of course, African Americans, both in the North and in the South, were loyal to the "Party of Lincoln" and consistently voted Republican. That changed in 1932, as blacks, like other Americans, deserted Hoover in favor of Roosevelt and his New Deal. The 1936 election was thus pivotal, for it solidified African American support for both FDR and the Democratic Party. That support was not inevitable. Roosevelt was never by any means an advocate for civil rights and never approached the commitment to civil rights shown by his wife. Katznelson, for instance, notes that "the New Deal permitted, or at least turned a blind eye toward, an organized system of racial cruelty."[76] Indeed, in the 1930s there was no clear difference on civil rights between the parties. The move of African Americans from affiliation with Republicans to support for the Democratic Party came as an indirect result of Roosevelt's economic policies.[77] This was practically accidental; FDR consistently argued that economics took precedence over racial justice.[78]

Roosevelt, for his part, was relatively indifferent to civil rights. He did not even make small changes when he could; the White House press corps, for instance, "operated within sharply defined racial limits."[79] Politically, he was hamstrung by the centrality of southern Democrats to the New Deal coalition and by their positions of influence as committee chairs in Congress.[80] Even had he been a stronger advocate for civil rights, it's doubtful he could have accomplished much given the institutional structures with which he had to contend.[81] It is perhaps important to note, however, that unlike many presidents, Roosevelt never denigrated African Americans. "One of the purposes of the present national Administration," he said in 1934 in a "Letter Urging the Fullest Opportunity for Exercise of the Right to Vote," "is to improve the lot of the men and women whose voices have not always been heard and whose welfare has not always been regarded by those in charge of our Government. The right to equality of treatment under that Government and in the choosing of that Government is inherent in democracy and its denial cannot anywhere be justified."[82] He may not have supported civil rights by advocating legislation, but he could find no principled reason to support Jim Crow either. FDR was consistently willing to accord African Americans a place in national symbolic life.[83] Such efforts seemed to promise presidential assistance in helping members of this important group share in the nation's material blessings. Little such effort was forthcoming.

The Depression disproportionately affected African Americans, especially in the South.[84] Southern blacks suffered the worst of the economic conditions; had the least help from state and local government; and, if that wasn't bad enough, were also subjected to increased violence and threats of violence. All these elements were evident in the case of the Scottsboro Boys.[85] The "Boys" were nine black teenagers, accused of rape in Alabama in 1931. All but one of them were convicted and sentenced to death. The initial trials were rushed, to say the least; the defendants' representation was weak. The national uproar resulted in a series of retrials, during which most of the convictions were overturned. In 1935, at the peak of the controversy, the Scottsboro case stood as a symbol of the national conversation, such as it was, on race: the unevenness of white justice; the potency of white fear; the possibility of communist agitation on behalf of African American rights; the unwillingness of the Supreme Court to intervene—all were on display.[86]

Cases like Scottsboro provided clear evidence, if such evidence was necessary, of the conditions African Americans faced in the American South. Northern blacks, however, suffered disproportionately as well and throughout the 1930s took major, sometimes crippling, decreases in wages.[87] Northern blacks lived primarily urban lives. Consequently, they were dependent on wages in ways that all city dwellers were, and the loss of factory jobs hit them particularly hard. Their difficulties were not much ameliorated by relief programs either. The New Deal was, more than any other previous program or set of programs, race neutral, at least in theory. In practice, most New Deal programs established racial classifications.[88] So African Americans were dependent on local officials to dispense relief fairly. It is unlikely that this occurred often, even in the relatively less discriminatory North.

The Roosevelt administration did make symbolic gestures toward African Americans. Roosevelt, for instance, established the Black Cabinet, a "loosely coordinated group of racial advisors on the staffs of various New Deal agencies and regular departments of government."[89] The Black Cabinet meant not only that African Americans had jobs in the administration (no small matter given the extent and duration of the Depression) but also that African American voices were heard, if not always attended to, when it came to matters of policy. Any such influence is not readily traceable, and the administration remained slow when it wasn't unyielding on racial politics.[90] But there was at least symbolic attention given to the demands of African Americans and some recognition that they had a right to make such demands. And make such demands they did. An article in the *Washington Weekly*, for example, noted that African American voters held "the balance of power in one or more states that Roosevelt must carry to renew his White House lease."[91] Certainly, machine bosses in the North were aware of the importance of this voting bloc. That African Americans voted so overwhelmingly for FDR is an important feature of this campaign, especially given the Democrats' relative lack of attention to the concerns of black voters.

In general, FDR, so willing to incorporate some interests into the federal government, left the interests of African Americans up to the states, a fact that was underlined by the role of the "Colored Division" in the 1936 election.[92] It is interesting, for instance, that the Women's Division is so well documented, in part a testament to Molly Dewson, of course. But by comparison, the material on the Colored Division is markedly limited and even somewhat random. In one file, for instance, there are patronage requests, letters advocating deportation of African Americans, press clippings on education, requests for meetings, and notes and letters from members of the NAACP. In short, anything that had to do with African American politics was bundled into a largely undifferentiated lump in the White House and in the DNC, with little effort made to consider how these various elements might reflect an important voting bloc or help those running the 1936 campaign to organize or mobilize that bloc.[93] There are in the files hints of a "Colored Democratic League" that appeared to operate independently of the DNC as well, but, again, the information is scanty; it does not seem to have been of much interest.[94]

There were, it should be noted, some efforts to reach African American voters. For example, one flier labeled *1933, the G.O.P Ship on the Rocks* features a drawing of a ship that had apparently rammed a rock. Below this is a drawing of a small home being foreclosed. Next to it a broadly grinning man is holding a paper that says, "Federal aid." The drawing is captioned, "Sixty colored farmers in each of the 1500 counties of the South have been loaned an average per capita of $200 for seed, fertilizer, livestock and machinery." The very bottom of the flier reads, "The Democratic Party saved the Nation and is now giving the Negro the squarest deal in its history. Will the Negro bite the hands that saved him? Answer Nov. 3."[95] African Americans were being reminded that this Roosevelt was even better than the Republican Roosevelt had been; his "deal" was even "squarer" than the one offered by his presidential cousin. African Americans should be grateful—like the man in the drawing, they should be happily smiling rather than giving in to animalistic urges to "bite." Having accepted federal largesse, they needed to reciprocate by voting for the president who had supported them. That support, it should be noted, was provided as economic aid. African Americans were understood to constitute an economically cohesive group. Race was depicted but also invisible. Extrapartisan forms of organization, potentially threatening to the political order, were not encouraged, and the Democratic Party was offered as the surest protection of African Americans. Economic claims could be recognized. Claims to civil rights were much less likely to be answered with governmental action.

Other fliers aimed at African American voters were equally explicit and underlined similar kinds of racial hierarchies. In one, a black farmer is depicted saying, "No need tellin' us what Roosevelt has done for the people—we know!" Another is on the phone, saying, "Pres Roosevelt! I'm about to lose my farm through a foreclosure—I understand the govt will help me!!" The caption asks, "Will the Negro desert the friend that saved him? Answer Nov. 3rd and vote the straight Democratic ticket."[96] African Americans were thus portrayed as primary beneficiaries of New Deal programs—they had direct access to their friend the president, and their farms had been saved by his direct intervention. Furthermore, African Americans were exhorted not just to vote for FDR but to vote a "straight Democratic ticket." In this instance, African American benefits were tied both to the president and to his party, a particularly interesting move given that party's overt and sustained commitment to Jim Crow.

In another example, in what appears to mimic a court summons, "Colored Voters" are "summoned to appear at your precinct on November 3, 1936, and cast your vote for your friend, your leader, and your President, Franklin D. Roosevelt, and upon your failure to appear at that time and place herein mentioned you will be liable for four long years of deprivation, starvation, and want for food, clothing, and shelter." Interestingly, this flier appears in the Labor Division files, possibly indicating that it was connected with efforts to mobilize the labor vote. And in this flier, unlike the ones that featured stereotypical drawings of African Americans, this one has no illustrations. Its arguments are all textual and grounded in class. The flier notes that "the moneyed interest is opposed to our friend, our leader, and our President." Further appeals argue that "colored war veterans received the bonus under this Administration. . . . Farmers never received any help from the Republican Administration compared to that given them under President Roosevelt."[97] The appeals here are clearly to economic self-interest. What FDR was unwilling to concede to race, he was willing to treat in terms of economics.

African Americans were also courted by the Women's Division and by extrapartisan organizations. Dewson sent a letter to her workers, noting, "This is a form letter, but please read it," reminding her state chairs that "we have a very active colored voters' division and some excellent colored speakers. . . . Nothing is so 100% in a campaign that you may not wish to speed up the work being done with the colored voters in your own state."[98] The Women's Division was, like most of the nation, segregated. It was also willing to dedicate at least some effort to African American voters in places where that vote was legal. The efforts of the Women's Division were supplemented by outreach by the GNL, which sought to better understand and to court African Americans. There are memos detailing the reasons why African Americans in the Midwest, for example, found themselves disappointed in the administration—such as low participation in the Civilian Conservation Corps; widespread discrimination in other New Deal programs, especially affecting white-collar workers; and the failure of the antilynching bill. These reasons were all policy based. It could therefore be assumed that policy would make a difference, and the memo's author was quick to offer policy-based solutions: elimination of discrimination, job training for African Americans, inclusion of African American farmers in New Deal programs, provision of housing, employment opportunities, and so on. The author also noted that "one feature kept in mind in these suggestions is that public opinion among Negroes is made by the White Collar Class. Therefore the measures suggested are intended to serve that class as well as the basic population."[99] Again, African Americans were presumed to have class interests in common; even when divided by class, the way to court them was by providing economic benefits, not political rights.

The GNL also recruited, and then lost, the support of Adam Clayton Powell, indicating it was, in fact, treating African Americans exactly like other Americans in at least one respect—it sought to influence the contours of public opinion through community leaders. In Powell's case, this effort proved fruitless. He initially accepted the chairmanship of the GNL's "Colored Committee" but was outraged when Bishop R. R. Wright was made co-chair. Adding to the insult was the lack of consultation prior to this appointment. Powell complained that "I was completely ignored" and resigned.[100] Such neglect of such an important leader is practically inexplicable if the campaign was serious about attracting African American voters. Luckily for Roosevelt, the GNL was a nonpartisan organization and only tangentially connected to the White House. Roosevelt was able to retain both Powell's loyalty and the votes of New York African Americans.

Despite the insensitivity the campaign showed in some respects, it was careful to document the potential of the black vote. Edgar O. Brown, for instance, produced a list of all northern cities with black populations greater than one thousand. He also included the black population by state "inclusive of all towns and cities, where Negroes participate fully as voters."[101] Tacitly acknowledging the futility of courting black votes in the Jim Crow South, advocates of African Americans instead looked for ways to earn northern black votes for the New Deal, thereby placing Roosevelt in their debt in a second term.

The Roosevelt campaign may not have been attentive to the needs and demands of individual leaders, and they may have been unwilling to offer much in the way of policy, but the little that they did do was still more than African

Americans had received under Republicans in the twentieth century. Under the New Deal, African Americans received symbolic affirmation and economic benefits. It was enough to gain their allegiance until the Roosevelt-appointed judges, as practically their last collective act, fundamentally altered race relations in the United States in the *Brown* decision, more than a decade away.[102] The Women's Division indicated the centrality of mobilizing members of some groups. The example of labor provides evidence for the necessity of both mobilizing and containing members of a potentially volatile group. African Americans present a group that was contained—by region and by the restriction of its interests to economics alone—and then gingerly mobilized. In all these cases, citizens were rendered more able to articulate political preferences and were also confined by group membership.

Conclusion

Through both its policy choices and its forms of campaign communication, the New Deal forged new understandings of political identity and capitalized on existing ones. Members of groups like women, wage workers, and African Americans were constituted as politically important and encouraged to press for their shared economic interests on the basis of those affiliations. These new understandings were, however, also premised on prevailing social norms. Thus, FDR could promote individual women and their interests as a group while doing so on the basis of specific, maternalist assumptions about women, their work, and their role in politics.[103] Because of the centrality of economics to the New Deal, labor was able to develop as an independent entity, strongly affiliated with, but not reliant on, the Democratic Party. African Americans, on the other hand, remained citizens in a "semi-feudal" state, dependent on state politics and generally unable to look to the federal government for help. The legacy of the New Deal, then, is one of both incorporation and division.[104]

Both those affiliations and the hierarchies that supported them were useful to the president and to his 1936 campaign, which used those identities as a means of mobilizing the mass public. As Jerome M. Mileur put it, "It was in the mobilization of new voters, the subtraction of others, and the conversion of yet others that the New Deal reorganized the lines of party combat in 1936 and redefined the battle around the role and responsibilities of the new liberal national state."[105] Roosevelt could offer members of groups what he could not offer individuals. He could argue that any group member who benefited from the New Deal benefited all group members—thus, by seeing themselves as members of groups, individuals were encouraged to satisfy their own self-interest and to see that self-interest as a form of citizenship.

Organizing the electorate into groups helped the 1936 Roosevelt campaign and the national government understand and accommodate (or not) the interests represented by those groups. Such organization thus increased access to government for some group members. It also reduced their ability as individuals to react to governmental actions and policies. Creating, for instance, a "laborer" when where a "citizen" once stood is necessarily a reductive move, no matter how much that laborer is encouraged to participate in politics.

These practices also reinforced old hierarchies. In the case of women, for instance, much of the success of the Women's Division was attributable to Dewson's personal energy and her ability to obtain a hearing for her ideas from Roosevelt himself. She wielded a great deal of personal influence. But when she left the Women's Division, its influence diminished. She had been unable to translate individual influence into lasting institutional power for women who still tended to be viewed as always and inevitably subordinate to men. In the case of labor, unions were both a means of organizing workers for their own ends and a means of controlling those workers. African Americans earned much less for their loyalty to the New Deal, at least in the short term, than either wage workers or women.[106] The price was paid in terms of rural voters, who, outside of the South at least, increasingly moved to the Republican ranks.[107] FDR's willingness to recognize the validity of these new identities and political demands based on them helped bring African Americans, women, and labor into the New Deal coalition in 1936. This recognition also helped forestall the growth of leftist political organizations in the United States—the election of 1936 all but destroyed the viability of the Socialist Party. Interest-group politics paid other dividends for the president: "Roosevelt systematized interest-group politics more generally to include many constituencies—labor, senior citizens, farmers, union workers. The president made groups where only individual citizens or isolated cranks had stood before, ministered to those groups, and was rewarded with votes."[108] By organizing the electorate as interest groups, he was able to both mobilize that electorate for campaigns and contain it once the campaign was over.

But as in the case of some of Roosevelt's other political mechanisms, structures that he created to help him govern outside of the political party also trapped him.[109] As the people, constituted as members of interest groups, came to understand that they could collectively influence the nature of public policies aimed at their interests, the number of such groups exploded, creating pressures with which institutional structures were ill prepared to deal. Increasingly, then, these structures came to be tailored to the needs of the individual executive, who was beholden to the people, not to the party. The more politics came to depend on an individual president's relationship with the mass public, the less stable the political world became. This dependence started with the modern presidential campaign.

4

SPEAKING FOR THE PUBLIC, EMPOWERING THE PRESIDENCY

One of the hallmarks of the rhetorical presidency, and certainly the one that has received the most scholarly attention, is the changed relationship it signals between the government and the governed.[1] That relationship had been continually modified over time, with important watersheds including the presidencies of Andrew Jackson, Abraham Lincoln, Woodrow Wilson, and the first Roosevelt. But few presidents were able to foster the kind of personal attachment—or the level of personal animosity—associated with FDR. Partly, of course, this is because no other president governed for as long as Roosevelt, and partly it has to do with the political context in which he governed. This new relationship, though, is also the product of an intentional strategy promulgated by the president himself. That strategy can be seen in various manifestations throughout his long presidency, but it is especially visible in the rhetoric of the 1936 campaign. Many presidents have used public opinion as a warrant for political action.[2] Roosevelt systematized that practice and grounded his political authority in the linkage between the people and their government, which joined each other in the office of the presidency. The relationship he established with the nation's people was thus deeply personal.

Thomas Farrell noted that, in addition to its economic effects, "the Great Depression challenged existing rhetorical conventions. It deflated symbolic resources and bankrupted political speaking." FDR's rhetorical problem in confronting the Depression was, then, both a problem of policy and a problem of political authority. According to Farrell, FDR addressed the latter problem by reconstituting the relationship between the governed and the government in terms of governmental responsibilities and duties and by depicting the nation as active, able to create reasonable responses to the crisis, and engaged in constructive collective rather than individually motivated action.[3] By the end of his time in office, FDR had united the nation as neighbors and argued for an essential, national self-understanding in place of the previously existing, and now bankrupt, reliance on the local.[4]

But by 1936 that barely established understanding was difficult to sustain, as the Depression continued and Roosevelt's personal authority seemed to weaken. So the administration relied on several tactics to assure the president's reelection, some organizational, others rhetorical.[5] Organizationally, as we have seen, he monitored public opinion and created structures designed to mobilize previously excluded voters. Rhetorically, he stressed national unity, emphasizing the benefits of his programs to the marginalized and weakest citizens, whom he characterized as agents with considerable power. On the other hand, he indicated in no uncertain terms the divisive potential of his opponents. A vote for Roosevelt became the mechanism through which the fragile national unity and national prosperity could be maintained.[6] A vote for Alf Landon and the Republicans, on the other hand (at least according to FDR), was sure to lead to a rupture of national unity and the further concentration of wealth in the hands of a few invidious individuals. The overarching argument extending over all these claims was that both the unity and the protection it afforded were weak and endangered. They depended on the presence of a strong national executive, dedicated to promulgating national unity based on the idea of widespread national inclusion. They depended, in short, on Roosevelt himself.

This chapter takes those arguments seriously, dealing first with Roosevelt's campaign rhetoric, which was organized around four basic premises: the centrality of presidential power; the importance of a national understanding of American politics; the need for government to assume responsibility for protecting its weakest and most vulnerable citizens; and a propensity for defining the Republican opposition as implacably opposed to all these factors and thus as inherently inimical to the national interest. I then briefly look at the ways in which his opposition sought to counter those claims and advance its own understanding of the route to national recovery. I conclude with the argument that Roosevelt's vision was powerful not least because it offered a simple and homey depiction of a united nation led by a strong president, blending the promise of security with the capacity for progress.⁷ He envisioned the national government as benevolent while suggesting that it increased the public's agency. In FDR's version of politics, an empowered people granted authority to the national government and its president.

This tactic both encouraged citizen participation in elections and government and also worked against it. FDR advanced the understanding of elections as deliberative occasions and always argued that citizens had the capacity to understand and make judgments about even the most complex policies. The overt paternalism of his position—that the nation's first priority was security and that only a strong president could achieve and protect that security—also encouraged citizens to leave political matters in the hands of the president, thus mitigating against participation and deliberation.⁸

The Roosevelt Campaign

Roosevelt had, above all, the advantage of incumbency and could thus, from the vantage point of Washington, D.C., concentrate on national administration rather than on a national campaign. He traveled little, spoke relatively infrequently, and capitalized on the media attention that was a consistent part of his presidency. As chief executive of a large and growing national government, FDR created news seemingly without effort. Republicans, as the out party, had to work considerably harder to earn the kind of national attention Roosevelt could take for granted. Moreover, the Democrats controlled both Congress and the presidency, which meant that they essentially controlled the policy-making process. They could initiate new programs, pass new legislation, or decline to do anything at all. Republicans could only react to Democratic decisions. This meant that they had little influence over the national agenda and in almost all matters of national import were placed in a defensive position—politically, therefore, in a weak position.⁹

No one knew better than FDR what to do with the political initiative. Publicly, he largely ignored the Republicans and indeed, the election, although, as we have seen, considerable effort was expended behind the scenes.¹⁰ That spring, the president conducted a "nonpolitical" tour of flood-damaged states, using the opportunity to make his presence felt, and in late June he delivered a speech at the Democratic convention, which was notable more for the controversy over the "two-thirds rule" than for any real challenge to the president.¹¹

While it is clear that his rhetoric throughout 1936 was directed at framing the campaign, for Roosevelt, and for much of the nation, the campaign didn't really begin until his speech at Syracuse University on September 29, 1936. While Roosevelt spent only a little time on the stump, his campaign constituted a remarkable performance.[12] In all his campaign speeches Roosevelt outlined the themes of the election and placed himself as the vital center of those themes. He defined himself as the hinge on which all political progress and security depended. Because he grounded this appeal in the will of the people, this rhetoric simultaneously declared that "the people" had agency and empowered the national government.

Presidential Power

Under Roosevelt the media and the presidency became more entwined and more mutually reinforcing than at any prior period in American history. Certainly, no previous president received as much publicity as did Roosevelt, who was prominently featured in newspapers, on the radio, in newsreels, and in magazines.[13] He was in the news for a reason. Under Roosevelt the presidency assumed a standing it had previously held only in times of war. Since 1932 the president had an expanded role in nearly every aspect of government: legislation, budgeting, and administration. Roosevelt considered that expansion a result of the work required by government—as government assumed increased responsibility for the nation's welfare, it also needed to grow. He argued that the growth was a sign not of incipient dictatorship, as his critics charged, but of improved democratic capacities. In the face of constant accusations concerning dictatorial power, that argument had to be made, and made again.

Roosevelt's 1936 State of the Union address is widely considered to be the opening salvo of the electoral battle, foreshadowing as it did many of the campaign's themes and specifically containing a defense of presidential power. He began this address with foreign policy, underlining the success of the Good Neighbor Policy and noting that the situation in Europe was becoming increasingly dangerous, containing "many of the elements that lead to the tragedy of general war." In this context, skilled leadership became increasingly important, as was the commitment of that leadership to American values: "I realize that I have emphasized to you the gravity of the situation which confronts the people of the world. The emphasis is justified because of its importance to civilization and therefore to the United States. Peace is jeopardized by the few and not by the many. Peace is threatened by those who seek selfish power."[14] First, note how he referenced the constellation of war, security, and presidential power. In foreign policy the president had both power and responsibility lacking in other contexts. Roosevelt had consistently talked about the national response to the Depression in military terms, so it wasn't much of a leap to argue that he also needed to extend wartime powers of the domestic context.

Note also how his criticism of those threatening peace in Europe is identical to his attacks on his domestic opponents. The problem in both foreign and domestic policy is the same: a few selfish, power-seeking individuals endanger the peace and the well-being of the community-minded many. Willing to find these forces on the home front, he was in favor of "well-ordered neutrality" internationally, but it was watchful neutrality.[15] His implication was clear. Arguing for a similarity of opponents, he was also arguing for similar means to combat them. The nation's security, both at home and abroad, depended on the president. It was thus imperative that he be given power appropriate to his task.

For Roosevelt, empowering the president served, rather than subverted, democracy. He argued that he was, in fact, much more committed to democracy than were Republicans. Under his leadership, "Government became the representative and the trustee of the public interest. Our aim was to build upon essentially democratic institutions, seeking all the while the adjustment of burdens, the help of the needy, the protection of the weak, the liberation of the exploited and the genuine protection of the people's property."[16] He argued that under his administration government had assumed both sides of the representative equation—it represented the people directly and functioned as trustee, watchfully guarding the national interest for the people. Its aim was not its own perpetuation nor the aggrandizement of a specific class but a fair apportionment of national burdens, with an eye toward the needs of the nation's most vulnerable members. Strong government was a tool for empowering a weak public.

He claimed that this task, like the task of representing democratic forms of government in the international arena, was risky. "To be sure," he said, "we have invited battle. We have earned the hatred of entrenched greed." Those who constituted the forces of that greed were the enemy—the metaphors were all martial; compromise was ruled out. Once war has been declared, the only option was victory. In domestic as in foreign affairs, the argument was the same: "Autocrats in small things, they seek autocracy in bigger things."[17] Roosevelt thus required wartime power to fight both foreign and domestic enemies—who, it turns out, were ideologically the same enemy. Autocrats in Europe sought territorial conquest. Autocrats at home were, for the moment, content with controlling the national economy. In both cases, the nation was best protected by a strong chief executive who understood how to recognize and counter autocracy—in the people's name.

Throughout the 1936 campaign then, he defended executive power as necessary for the protection of the people's empowerment. Political power concentrated in the hands of a strong chief executive was required to counter the economic power concentrated in the hands of his opponents. Because "our country is indeed passing through a period which is urgently in need of ardent protectors of the rights of the common man," he argued, "the American citizen could appeal only to the organized power of Government."[18] That organized power properly belonged in the hands of the president, whose avowed task was to use that power to protect the national interest.

Thus, FDR likened his task as president to that of Andrew Jackson: "To most of us, Andrew Jackson appropriately has become the symbol of certain great ideals. I like best to think of him as a man whom the average American deeply and fundamentally understood. To the masses of his countrymen, his purposes and his character were an open book. They loved him well because they understood him well—his passion for justice, his championship of the cause of the exploited and the downtrodden, his ardent and flaming patriotism."[19] Roosevelt gave his audience the terms through which he wanted to be seen and judged—like Jackson, he should be well understood and well loved and for the same reasons—both presidents were dedicated patriots who understood that patriotism as encompassing protection of "the exploited and the downtrodden." There was nothing hidden or malign in their actions; both presidents were "an open book," visible and thus intelligible to their constituents.

He defined his task as fundamentally protective and implied that if the Republicans were restored to power, that protection would be unavailable; the public interest would no longer be the focus of government; the weak, the exploited, and the needy would again be vulnerable. Here FDR mixed retrospective and prospective voting appeals, inviting the public to remember the past—both prior to his administration and during its first years—and also inviting them to project a return to pre–New Deal conditions as a result of a return to Republican administration. This rhetoric reflected the frequent association of campaigns and battle metaphors. It also created a political problem, for when the opposition in an election is labeled the enemy, postelection reconciliation becomes much more difficult. Roosevelt offered his own solution to this problem, claiming that his election would result in the annihilation of the forces of selfishness; Republicans as well as Democrats would be purified. In offering this rhetoric of purification, he gave both purpose and meaning to the organizational strategies of the administration's campaign. The president argued that such organization was needed to facilitate his leadership, which was designed to promote national unity.

One Nation, Indivisible

Roosevelt argued throughout the campaign that the nation under the Republicans had been divided into the haves and have-nots, the weak and the strong. It was also characterized by sectional divisions, by rifts based on religion, by rural-urban conflict; everywhere he looked he saw a divided nation. Under his leadership, he claimed, a new national unity had been born, overcoming all these divisions in a spirit of national community based on a shared commitment to specific values. No matter their region, class, race, or religion, all Americans were equally dedicated to their shared national life. That shared commitment was endangered by the kind of selfishness, narrowness, and parochialism that characterized his opposition. He said, "A century ago this country was regarded as an economic unity. But as time went on, things happened. The country, bit by bit, was cut up into segments. We heard, more and more, about the problems of particular localities, the problems of particular groups. More and more people put on blinders; they could see only their own individual interests or the single community in which their business happened to be located."[20] The Republicans, the party of limited vision, could not see the problem clearly. Wearing blinders, they could only contribute to national problems. The Democrats, under Roosevelt, had greater clarity of vision. They could both see and act on the true national interest. Electing Roosevelt was therefore the best way to promote national unity, and national unity was the best way to empower the nation's citizens. Having organizationally segmented the nation into various groups to mobilize and contain them, this rhetoric united members of those groups as actors in a common enterprise.

On "Brotherhood Day," for instance, FDR gave a radio address in which he noted, "The National Conference on Jews and Christians has set aside a day on which we can meet, not primarily as Protestants or Catholics or Jews but as believing Americans; a day on which we can dedicate ourselves not to the things which divide us but to the things which unite us." For Roosevelt, the whole purpose of citizenship was this dedication to unity rather than division: "The very state of the world is a summons to us to stand together."[21] A campaign that individualized the public as neighbors and segmented them on the basis of group affiliation united them as a presidential constituency.

This unity, he argued, was possible because of shared commitment to national values, strongly associated with the Judeo-Christian tradition. Those values and that tradition provided the glue connecting the entire nation: "I like to think of our country as one home in which the interests of each member are bound up with the happiness of all," he said.[22] So for him, the real enemy was national division fomented by selfishness—by a failure to realize that the nation was a shared home in which its citizens were interconnected and interdependent. Selfishness disempowered the public. Unity under his leadership empowered it as well as providing security in an unstable world.

Roosevelt's campaign was thus premised on both the conservative argument of the stability of shared values and the progressive one of the importance of adapting to a changing world. For instance, speaking to a group of Young Democrats, the president said, "The world in which millions of you have come of age is not the set old world of your fathers. Some of yesterday's certainties have vanished; many of yesterday's certainties are questioned . . . because the facts and needs of civilization have changed more greatly in this generation than in the century which preceded us." Some of "yesterday's certainties"—those related to national values—were worth preserving. Others were appropriately gone or questioned. Some conditions—those "that make employment and opportunity possible"—merited restoration. Others, such as those that inhibited efficiency, for example, were no longer useful and should not be recalled. But the American spirit, that powerful force of national unity, remained constant and important: "And make no mistake about it—the same qualities of heroism and faith and vision that were required to bring the forces of nature into subjugation will be required—in even greater measure—to bring under proper control the forces of modern society."[23] Roosevelt thus conjured the pioneer to argue for constancy amid change, making the case that some change was necessary and valuable but that some elements remained constant and invariable and had to be guarded and preserved, for they alone could provide the grounding for national unity. For those elements to be maintained, it was important that the nation include everyone, especially those most vulnerable to changing material conditions.

Protecting the Marginalized

Despite his attacks on Republicans, Roosevelt's appeals to those who felt disenfranchised were specifically nonpartisan and strongly personalized.[24] He announced that his audience was the nation, not the party, an appeal made more plausible by the fact of incumbency.[25] His nation was not torn by divisive partisanship but was united by its widely shared adherence to specific values: "a sense of fair play among men . . . their essential dependence upon one another . . . a sense of equality among men . . . freedom in pursuit of truth."[26] These values, which were vague enough to prevent fundamental opposition, were also useful ways to constitute his audience as the national electorate. If Roosevelt was for these values, Republicans must perforce be opposed to them. Democrats stood for equality and fair play; their opponents therefore represented special privilege of the sort that caused the Depression and imposed its effects disproportionately on the poor.

This ostensibly nonpolitical appeal was underlined by the work of the Good Neighbor League and the Committee of One. It was also validated when former Republicans joined his campaign. One such Republican, Stanley High, wrote an essay for the *Forum* in May 1936, arguing that, contrary to all the campaign rhetoric, the election was not about Roosevelt as a person. It was about Roosevelt insofar as he embodied "a certain tendency in American life." High asserted that "the New Deal is by no means all it ought to be," but also that "for the first time the American government has begun to assume—as the governments of most civilized nations have done for many years—that the economic well-being of the people is a matter for executive and legislative action." For High, that principle was associated with Roosevelt, and its imperatives required the president's reelection. He noted that "big business men" opposed the New Deal, implying the immensity of the opposition. These "big" capitalists, for High, "were not against the idea that the hungry should be fed. They were complaining about only the fact that the New Deal had gone ahead and fed them." In other matters as well, the opposition "could not forgive Mr. Roosevelt's attempt to turn these statements [of widely shared principles] into policies." High argued that the whole purpose of the New Deal was inclusion. It aimed "to provide a more widespread security for the masses of the American people."[27] This, in a nutshell, was the keystone of the Democratic campaign: it pitted the "masses of the American people" against the few "big business men." It was a contest of the many against the few, with the soul of the nation as the prize.

Explicit and implicit appeals to class characterized most of Roosevelt's rhetoric in 1936.[28] Making his implicit appeals, Roosevelt argued, "Automatic Machinery, the device of corporate ownership, the monumental accumulations of capital—these are some of the factors that have made it necessary for our country and its Government to look at men and measures from a new point of view, seeking new means for the restoration of equality of opportunity."[29] Note that he depicted his actions as restorative, not revolutionary. FDR claimed to be returning the nation to a state of economic equality, not proposing radical new ideas. Note also his use of distanced, even passive language. The developments he speaks of merely occurred—in Kenneth Burke's terms, they constituted the scene of the action; there is no observable agent.[30] This means that there was no one to blame; external forces created the problems Roosevelt identified. Since there was no perpetrator, only the scene of capitalism bore responsibility. Thus members of all classes had a common interest in addressing the common problems created by that scene.

This strategy worked in part because Roosevelt himself did not argue in terms of a set of fixed and immutable classes perpetually at war. Like everything else in his political world, FDR assumed fluidity among classes and among the people who populated them. He was infinitely more likely to argue that politics was a contest among organized interests, which he understood as temporary amalgamations, than a static battle between immutable classes.[31] The point was to provide protection for the members of all classes so that they could argue over the national interest from a sound basis of equality: "In our national life, public and private, the very nature of free government demands that there must be a line of defense held by the yeomanry of business and industry and agriculture. I do not mean the generalissimos, but the small men, the average men in business and industry and agriculture—those who have an ownership in their business and a responsibility which give them stability. Any elemental policy, economic or political, which tends to eliminate these dependable defenders of democratic institutions, and to concentrate control in the hands of a few, small, powerful groups, is directly opposed to the stability of government and to democratic government itself."[32] National stability, like international stability, was not brought about by relying on "generalissimos" but by protecting the average person—who had a sense of ownership and thus of responsibility to the overall health of the polity rather than an exploitive interest in it. Again, Roosevelt's conception of democratic citizenship was clear. Not only were average people central to governmental policy (it existed for them), but they were also central participants in governmental processes (policy was made by them). Under his leadership, that conception of politics would be protected and enacted through a strong national government.

Roosevelt consistently argued that American capitalism was not a zero-sum game, but that his vision of a "more abundant life" could be—and should be— widely shared. The mechanism for sharing was not the market but the national government. "Building national income and distributing it more widely, mean not only bettering of conditions of life, but the end of, and insurance against, individual and national deficits in the days to come. Nationwide thinking, nationwide planning, and nationwide action are the three great essentials to prevent nationwide crises for future generations to struggle through."[33] Government existed to serve as mediator among the nation's various interests. Roosevelt thus promulgated the segmentation of citizenship and simultaneously offered his own leadership as a way of unifying and empowering the nation.

This was an especially important idea in the politics of the mid-1930s, when revolution seemed possible and when the mechanisms of private markets had so clearly failed. For Roosevelt, government could endure only if it also succeeded in providing at least minimal security for its citizens.[34] Roosevelt and his surrogates pounded this message home. Molly Dewson, for instance, gave a radio address answering Republican attacks on Social Security and arguing, "Age has its compensations. Abundant compensations. But there is no physical compensation for an empty stomach. There is no mental compensation for the torture of being the unpaying, perhaps the unwanted, guest in someone else's home."[35] This combination of affirmation, understanding, and security, coming from an older woman, had broad potential appeal and underlined the implicit claim that the Republicans, who opposed Social Security, were unfeeling and unconcerned for the difficult position in which many citizens continued to find themselves. The national press also picked up this theme, noting that Roosevelt's challenge was to provide security "without relinquishing those historic civil liberties brought with the dear blood and bones of our Anglo Saxon ancestors."[36] The campaign was premised, here as elsewhere, on the idea that the Democrats cherished the nation's traditional values but also understood that the application of those values had to adapt to changing political and economic contexts. Those changes included a broader application of security and the benefits of national life. The campaign communication thus created a specific sense of inclusive and empowered citizenship and argued that the Republicans defended an exclusive and exclusionary understanding of the national polity in which one class reaped the benefits and another paid the price.

Making the Case

Roosevelt's campaign relied on both an affirmative and a negative case for his reelection. On the positive side, FDR argued consistently that the state, led by a strong executive, had an important role in providing for the "general welfare" and that this was both constitutional and important.[37] National unity required this role, for without the national government the balance of interests could not be properly maintained and the weak and vulnerable would suffer. The Democrats, under Roosevelt's leadership, were consistently depicted in the national campaign as the party most able to facilitate national unity through its superior understanding of national values and the appropriate balance among competing interests. Roosevelt's opponents, because they favored narrow interests above the nation as a whole, represented a danger to national unity.

Roosevelt thus offered explicit arguments identifying and excluding those who acted against the national interest in favor of their own self-interest. As his leadership faced challenges in 1936, he moved toward the "view that some well-chosen enemies might actually be a help in underpinning the enthusiasm of the majority."[38] Naturally, FDR placed the blame for negative campaigning on his opponents, noting in the introduction to the 1936 volume of his *Public Papers* that "through the Spring, every effort was made by the opposition to attack individuals, to magnify minor errors of administration, to misrepresent actual facts, and at the same time to give lip service to the cause of social betterment and elimination of ancient abuses, without offering any specific proposals alternative to the methods we were following."[39] The Republican opposition was depicted as prone to personal attacks, hitting below the political belt. They were guilty of distortion, dishonesty, and failure to propose specific plans. All this behavior was exercised in an effort to discredit the Roosevelt administration and return themselves to power. Republicans, he reminded his audience, "seek the restoration of their selfish power. They offer to lead us back round the same old corner into the same old dreary street."[40] They sought not the restoration of economic equality as FDR did, but the restoration of their own prosperity at the expense of the national, common interest. The "economic royalists" were interested only in their "new dynasties" and in their "thirsting for power, reached out for control over Government itself."[41] They were the incipient dictators dedicated to antidemocratic ideals. Roosevelt was all that stood between the American people and the return to monarchial principles.

Roosevelt's most devastating critiques were also his most accessible. In September 1936, officially opening his campaign at the Democratic State Convention in Syracuse, New York, the president said, "In the summer of 1933, a nice old gentleman wearing a silk hat fell off the end of a pier. He was unable to swim. A friend ran down the pier, dived overboard and pulled him out, but the silk hat floated off with the tide. After the old gentleman had been revived, he was effusive in his thanks. He praised his friend for saving his life. Today, three years later, the old gentleman is berating his friend because the silk hat was lost."[42] In one memorable anecdote, Roosevelt made the case for his reelection and against his opponents. They were rich, soft, and spoiled. They cared only about their own well-being and were guilty of base ingratitude as well as selfishness. Above all, they were laughable, not to be taken seriously. Throughout the campaign, Roosevelt took obvious pleasure in making fun of the ungrateful rich, who became targets of his more colorful invective.[43]

In depicting his opposition, Roosevelt turned the rhetorical tables on them. The Republicans' most potent charge against FDR was that the Democrats were threatening the constitutional order. They insisted that Roosevelt was an incipient dictator whose actions, even if well intended, destroyed national liberty. Roosevelt and his surrogates countered this set of arguments by defending presidential and governmental power as grounded in national values and essential to their continued protection. The nation, in this depiction, was threatened by autocracy abroad and by those who secretly yearned to establish autocracy at home. The protection of a strong chief executive, who understood and valued the average citizen, was required to stave off both threats.

This rhetoric was consistent with every other element of the campaign. The understanding of public opinion generated by polls and anecdotal evidence provided the administration with a detailed, varied, and rich understanding of how the mass public understood Roosevelt, the New Deal, and the nation.[44] This understanding infused the grassroots campaigns orchestrated by the Good Neighbor League and the Women's Division. Roosevelt's rhetoric ran through it all, explicating the purpose of his campaign in general in ways that resonated with the public mood. A number of forces drove Roosevelt to the left in 1936, but he went only so far as the needs of coalition building required. More important, as president he garnered more attention and wielded more interpretive power than his opponents, and his rhetoric thus set the frame for the campaign. Republicans were thrown onto the defensive and never gained interpretive traction in the campaign. The manifold weaknesses of their campaign made a difficult situation worse.

Opposing Roosevelt

Roosevelt's class appeals, as bombastic as they were, were also not entirely without merit. Republicans outspent Democrats in 1936 by a fairly large margin, and there is evidence that the financial contributions to the parties reflected fairly clear demarcations based on class.[45] As a result of New Deal policies and Rooseveltian rhetoric, many considered the administration dangerously antibusiness, a tendency that both mystified and aggravated the president.[46] While there was no "banker's revolt" in 1936, as is sometimes charged, it is true that bankers in general did not support FDR.[47] Bankers were not alone. Knowing what we now know about Roosevelt and his political success, it is easy to forget that there were always a significant number of Americans who opposed him and his policies.[48] He was also opposed by a number of newspapers, on both the Right and the Left.

The Republicans were therefore not without hope in 1936, at least not until the campaign began. Their strategy centered on trying to peel off as much of Roosevelt's 1932 support as possible, hoping to render those election results anomalous. Consequently, Republicans targeted conservative business interests, disaffected midwestern farmers angered by the Agricultural Adjustment Act, and those concerned about the increase in federal—and presidential—power.[49] They based their campaign on largely negative appeals, making it clear that they opposed Roosevelt and all his works, but being considerably less clear on the subject of what they actually supported. Like the president, his opponents focused on the president himself, portraying FDR as a dangerous radical, dedicated to usurping power, abrogating the Constitution, and destroying the American way of life.[50] Their best case for this would have been Roosevelt's plan for the Supreme Court, but on this the president remained determinedly silent, and thus the Republican argument became a series of accusations with little actual evidence.[51]

Given the organization and effort that the Democrats had been putting into the election and given their candidate's rhetorical ability, the opposition campaign would have been difficult enough, although continued economic difficulties gave Republicans at least one potential wedge, and Roosevelt's controversial actions provided another. The exploitation of those wedges, however, demanded carefully crafted and managed messages, and in 1936 the Right was neither well organized nor well disciplined. Conservatives were united mostly by their shared hatred for Franklin Roosevelt, but they did not agreed on the best way to attack him. The party was fractured and inchoate, and its leaders were apparently unable to unite behind any one person or set of clear policies. They did not want to reinvigorate the specter of Herbert Hoover, but had no other clear alternative to the policies so disastrously associated with his presidency. After a messy convention, they nominated a compromise (but by no means a consensus) candidate, who then failed to make a persuasive national case. Landon's absence left a space soon filled by a raucous collection of anti-Roosevelt voices, most of whom did more damage to their own base than to the Democrats. No group made more public noise or caused more self-inflicted wounds to Roosevelt's opposition than the American Liberty League.

The American Liberty League

After the massive Republican defeat in the 1934 midterm elections, businessmen formed the American Liberty League to protect the Constitution from the radicalism it associated with the New Deal. Men like DuPont executive and former Roosevelt supporter John Jacob Raskob and William H. Stayton grounded their arguments in principles like constitutionalism and individual liberty.[52] Others were more obviously personally invested in attacking Roosevelt.[53] Whatever arguments they made about principle, members of the Liberty League were opposed, often personally and sometimes obscenely, to the president himself.[54] This animosity was less important, however, than the league's apparent commitment to rolling back any reforms designed to help the poor, which bolstered the president's argument that he represented the nation's best security against a return to a disempowered people controlled by an exploitative government. One supporter, for instance, wrote the president, "I recently heard a prominent Republican say (*not for publication*) that the American Liberty League is doing more to insure your reelection than any other one single factor!"[55] Roosevelt was both fortunate in his enemies and willing to depict them in starkly negative terms. The league's communicative strategy seemed designed to lend credibility to Roosevelt's claims and made life very difficult indeed for the more mainstream elements of the Right. Landon's supporters were forced to spend valuable time and effort explaining away the league's actions and disassociating themselves from the league. Meanwhile Roosevelt and the Democrats were gleefully busy tying that particular albatross firmly around Alf Landon's neck.

Alf Landon and the Republicans

The Republican nomination had been hotly contested, which tended to split the party, while the Democrats were able to rally around their candidate much sooner and infinitely more happily. The Republican convention had been characterized by a lengthy contest between conservatives who represented very different versions of that philosophy: William Borah, Hiram Johnson, and Gifford Pinchot. This meant that Landon's candidacy appeared relatively controversial as the Republicans fought one another, while Roosevelt remained serenely above political matters and left campaigning to his surrogates, such as Henry Wallace, Homer Cummings, and the vituperative Harold Ickes.[56] Molly Dewson also represented Roosevelt on a tour of the western states and gave five radio addresses, all of which were dedicated to countering the Republican narrative.[57] The Democrats thus began campaigning against the Republicans before the Republicans established their campaign. Republicans could make no charges that were not immediately countered and never had the opportunity to define the terms of the debate—those terms had been definitively set by the White House long before the Republicans even had a candidate.

That candidate, once he managed to control the convention, proved unable to seize definitional control of the wider contest. Landon was a moderate Republican with a record of supporting many New Deal programs. He also had a strong record of civil rights and a well-deserved reputation for political courage. In agreement with many of Roosevelt's philosophical precepts, he was also connected to the values of thrift and self-reliance, which were potentially useful, especially when contrasted to the reasonably prevalent fears that the New Deal was wasteful, favored security over individualism, and emphasized social rights over social obligations.[58] Republicans were hopeful that Landon could attract the votes of disaffected Democrats and recapture the allegiance of the Progressive Midwest.

Had he dedicated himself to making that case, he might have done so. Landon was, however, all but absent in the early days of the campaign. While Roosevelt kept himself firmly before the public under the auspices of his "nonpolitical" tour, Landon was virtually invisible. In a time when campaigns were increasingly public and mass-oriented, Landon's case was not being made in the most important venues. His relative silence left all the more room for the media to concentrate on the wild charges associated with the Liberty League and further undermined the Republican ability to gain any control over the campaign.

When Landon did speak, it was without the wide range of communicative skills the president could command. His speech accepting the Republican nomination was a clear, concise, and uninspiring argument, grounded in his promise to keep the oath of office "inviolate," implying that his administration, unlike Roosevelt's, would be conducted in accordance with constitutional principles. He promised to "approach the issues fairly, as I see them, without rancor or passion," a claim that may well have relieved those Republicans who had been suffering from the excesses associated with the Liberty League.[59] Where FDR combined his emphasis on the reasoning ability of the electorate with appeals demonstrating his empathy with national suffering and promises to restore national security, Landon's rhetoric stressed reason but lacked both the empathy and the reassurance of the president's.

Landon argued, for example, that "no people can make headway where great numbers are supported in idleness. There is no future in relief rolls." For those Americans whose survival depended on government employment or those rolls, this must have had an ominous sound. Roosevelt had always argued that relief was not to be preferred in general; it was only to be preferred to the continuance of national distress. Landon made no such provision. He argued instead that "the law of this world is that man shall eat bread by the sweat of his brow," implying that those who accepted relief were unwilling to work rather than entertaining the more charitable possibility that they had been unable to find it.[60]

Landon did better with the argument that Roosevelt promised to restore national security but had failed to do so. He charged the Roosevelt administration with ineffective economic policies and with following an uncertain, wavering, and inconsistent path toward it, arguing that, "as a result, recovery has been set back again and again. This was not all of the failure. Practical progressives have suffered the disheartening experience of seeing many liberal objectives discredited during the past three years by careless thinking, unworkable laws, and incompetent administration."[61] According to Landon, Roosevelt, and not the Republicans, had been discredited; the administration had been both impractical and incompetent. Relief had proven destructive, recovery derailed, and, apparently, reform unnecessary. According to Landon, all three prongs of the New Deal, then, had failed.

Having indicted Roosevelt, Landon attempted to alter the terms of the national debate. "For it must be remembered that the welfare of our people is not recorded on the financial pages of the newspapers. It cannot be measured in stock market prices. The real test is to be found in the ability of the average American to engage in business, to obtain a job, to be a self-supporting and self-respecting member of his community."[62] Where FDR had premised national health on the strength of national community, united and sustained by common values, Landon argued that it was found in the market—in the premises of national economic hierarchies, in which all citizens were able to work and protect themselves but in which the government was absent. Roosevelt argued that the government had an important role. Landon, seeking governmental power, apparently did so to reduce the role of that government.[63]

By concentrating on business rather than the government, however, Landon also seemed to be restricting the hope of recovery to those most able to profit in the short term. Others would have to wait until the economy had recovered enough to provide jobs. Landon understood the New Deal as offering "incessant governmental intimidation and hostility," a claim that surely resonated with his immediate audience but also had the potential to threaten the mass of voters suspicious of business and fearful that Republicans would cut relief. To be sure, Landon promised to "aid these innocent victims of the depression," but this promise also required that citizens see themselves as victims. Recall that the overwhelming message of Roosevelt's campaign was aimed at citizens understood as agents—they were fully able to understand complex issues and to act on that understanding. Depicting them as victims robbed them of agency. Limiting the power of government robbed them of the mechanism through which the Democrats promised they could exercise that agency. In an electoral battle that centered on the role of the government and in which these terms had been laid out, this response was not likely to garner many votes from the areas in which the Republicans most clearly needed them.

The campaign suffered from one other problem: the decision to attack Social Security.[64] Social Security had done more than any other program to earn or recapture the allegiance of the nation's most vulnerable citizens.[65] Attacking that program thus seemed to validate all the Democratic charges against the Republicans, confirming that they were selfish, greedy, and fundamentally opposed to the interests of the working classes. While Landon argued that if given time, social security would be rendered unnecessary by the fact of recovery driven by Republican management, the memory of the results of recent Republican management and the absence of what we now call the "safety net" was too painful for many Americans to wish a return to conditions in which they had come to think of themselves as vulnerable to the depredations of the economically powerful. For them, Republican promises were more worrying than reassuring.

If the campaign had come down to a question of which party was better able to manage a system of enlarged government, the Republicans might well have done better than they did. But accepting these terms would also have been tantamount to a defeat of Republican principles of small government, healthy markets, and a stress on the centrality of individual liberty. In 1936 those principles were still associated with the economic crisis and, perhaps more important, with the indifference to suffering with which that crisis had apparently been met by the Republicans. Voters were in no hurry to invite a return to those principles or the conditions with which they associated them. Still, had Landon spoken more frequently, or more forcefully, making the case for national economy and good management within a context of protection for the unemployed, his campaign might have resonated with a larger audience. But constrained by the position in which Republicans found themselves, his campaign rhetoric was uninteresting and uninspiring. But it was considerably better than the appeals offered by other Roosevelt detractors during the campaign.

The Politics of Fear

Not only did Landon have to contend with the sour legacy of the Liberty League, but immediately after his nomination he faced further opposition from some of his own presumptive supporters. Gerald Smith and Father Coughlin split with the Republicans and formed the short-lived and impressively ineffective Union Party, dedicated to "defeating Franklin Roosevelt and 'the communistic philosophy of Frankfurter, Ickes, Hopkins and Wallace.'"[66] They had grandiose ideas about the extent of their support and a tendency to insist on the most outlandish claims available concerning the politics and policies of the president and his staff. More absurd than even the most absurd fulminations of the Liberty League, the Union Party made considerable noise and no political headway, but it contributed to the impression that the Right had lost all credibility and thus made Landon's task all the more difficult.[67]

The administration kept track of these charges, and the files at the Roosevelt Library contain pamphlets with titles such as *Now Who's Un-American?* (an exposé of communism in government by a group called the American Indian Federation), a flyer on antivivisection, and various other flyers "connecting" Roosevelt to the worst excesses of the USSR.[68] These flyers and pamphlets provide a useful contrast to the Democrats, for the Democratic campaign material stressed the importance of "facts" and encouraged a conception of citizenship as informed and reasoning. That material assumed that all citizens were capable of understanding and participating in political debate. When FDR wielded anger, it was to depict the president as a fighter for the "forgotten man," and the animosity was directed at those who were seen as a common enemy.[69] Landon offered a vision of politics that also considered voters as reasoning and reasonable, but he lacked Roosevelt's emotive capacity. Opposition material, as it was collected by the DNC, on the other hand, seems to encourage a sense of citizenship motivated primarily by fear. Roosevelt and his surrogates wielded humor and stressed empathy. They made a clear and consistent case for the president's reelection. Apart from Landon, Roosevelt's opponents seemed unable to stop relying on anger, which often seemed directed at the very citizens whose support they were seeking. It is notable, for instance, that the pamphlet put out by the Reorganization Committee of the Republican Party of Cook County, Illinois, lists a series of "demands" and deploys a strident tone throughout, detailing those demands and the commitments connected to them. Even at this historical distance there is something a bit off-putting in the rhetorical vigor of this pamphlet.[70]

Apart from the calmly reasoned arguments made by the Republicans' standard-bearer, this tone was pervasive. In April 1936 the Honorable George Wharton Pepper delivered an address to the Republican Women's Luncheon Club of Philadelphia, in which he pointed to "the vast army of political mercenaries on the federal pay roll, to the immense political possibilities of huge funds spent in the name of relief and to the difficulty of debunking the President's policies in such fashion as to make everybody realize that there is poison in the jam." Such rhetoric made the Republican case both in content and by implication: Roosevelt and the New Deal were dishonest, they were destroying the national budget for political purposes, and the national interest was likewise at stake. Pepper insisted that principled argument was difficult in such a context, for people were unable to see the long-term dangers because they were so focused on short-term personal gain. According to Pepper, the president had, in Lewis Carroll's words, "charmed them with smiles and with soap."[71] Those citizens were apparently willing to be so charmed.

In contrast to such charm, Pepper offered a detailed argument of the proper functioning of the American constitutional system. His view was explicitly paternalistic. He argued for a president who "has in a very real sense the capacity to be a father of his people," unlike FDR, who "is in no real sense a President of the United States; he is an astute leader of a group within a group, and his policies are not national policies but class policies." Pepper admitted to having his "blood boil" at the lack of "honor and integrity" he found in Roosevelt, and he likewise opposed the president's "recklessness."[72] Apparently oblivious to the thought that in condemning the president he was also condemning those who supported him, Pepper implied that those citizens were either dupes or collaborators.

Pepper's use of the specter of "regimentation," the loss of essential liberties, and the disrespect FDR was said to have toward the other institutions of government was at least potentially likely to resonate with those voters who worried about the cost of the New Deal (and as we saw in the clergy letters, those voters were certainly out there), but those appeals appear only after the more ad hominem attacks; they tend to read as piled-on rather than reasoned arguments. There is such a flurry of arguments, in fact, that the personal and political are thoroughly mixed. It is hard to tell if the speaker objects to the policies because they are Roosevelt's or if he objects to Roosevelt because he supports these policies.[73] The speech is thus very good evidence that it was the person of the president who stood at the center of this campaign.

This was a single campaign speech, and like many campaign speeches, its objective was doubtless to mobilize the faithful and perhaps convert the opposition. But it was also representative of the kind of arguments the Republicans made, and it thus reveals the weaknesses of the Republican case. In short, that case was defensive and angry in tone; it looked to the past, which most Americans, still in the midst of Depression, did not regard as a particularly good model for the future; it assumed that the voters were either victims of a manipulative campaign or greedy advocates of policies designed to supplant the national interest with narrow self-interest than fully reasoning citizens exercising good judgment based on principle; and it assumed that "a fatherly attitude toward all the people" would be better for the nation than an equal, who treated the citizens as "my friends" and who invited them to reason along with him. Equally important, the Republican campaign lacked both the charm and the humor that were part of most of Roosevelt's campaign appearances. More problematic was the resentment Pepper displayed toward any policies that smacked of redistribution, arguing that the New Deal was "designed to re-make the world so that it will be knave-proof and fool-proof."[74] His audience members were clearly among the privileged, but the idea that those who needed governmental assistance were knaves or fools rather than empowered citizens temporarily deprived of jobs because of the Depression was not one that was likely to have wide appeal.[75] Roosevelt offered a vision of his power and that of the presidency in general as essential to the restoration of American national security and the political agency of the American mass public. His opponents assailed that vision and in doing so seemed also to assail the vision of an empowered mass public.

Conclusion

Both Roosevelt and his opponents put the president at the heart of the 1936 campaign, and that election proved to be a national referendum on his leadership and of the activist role the federal government was increasingly assuming.[76] Republicans also placed the president at the heart of the election. Roosevelt argued that his leadership was essential to the "true" enactment of democracy in the United States and that his presidency was grounded in attention to the will of the people. He was, he claimed, their advocate, their protector, and their voice.

He expended considerable energy understanding and influencing public opinion. He used a variety of means, across a variety of media, to set the frame for the election. He also directed intense efforts aimed at organizing and mobilizing voters. Finally, he connected all these efforts in a well-conceived, coherent, and consistent campaign aimed at interpreting the state of the nation and his commitment to it. He offered the voters an important national role as well, defining them as reasoning participants in an important national debate. He offered a vision of a national community united in the face of foreign and domestic threats and empowered with the will to remain secure despite those threats.

Roosevelt's opponents, on the other hand, seemed largely incapable of overcoming their rage at Roosevelt and the nation that supported him. The splenetic outpourings of Herbert Hoover, Al Smith, and Father Coughlin drowned out the more balanced arguments offered by the Republican candidate. But even in its more temperate iterations, the Republican case was reduced to arguing for something that looked too much like a return to the conditions that most blamed for the Depression in the first place.

Interestingly, Roosevelt argued for unity, but his approach was to treat the audience as individual members of variously defined groups. While his appeals were most memorably based on class, the importance of region and religion should not be overlooked.[77] Roosevelt carried all income groups except the one at the top; he had little support among business or professional people. But his popularity among the middle and lower classes and among blue-collar workers in particular more than made up for that. He had little success among his fellow Protestants but was overwhelmingly popular with Catholics, Jews, and those without religious affiliation.[78] He carried the urban North by impressive margins—in those areas that had increasing population and that were increasingly important in the developing nation, FDR and the Democrats had the strongest appeal.

Partly, this was because FDR ran a campaign that did not emphasize partisanship or party lines but relied on a crusading appeal directed at reinventing the liberal state.[79] Most important, that election providing a convincing warrant for the connection between a strong presidency and centralized governmental power, and a dependence on public opinion as a source of the legitimacy of both. The legitimacy of those connections had limits, and Roosevelt would learn something about those limits as a result of his failures to pack the Supreme Court and purge Congress. But the continued use of connections made by FDR in 1936 proved to be a lasting consequence of his style of governance and the changes he authorized in the structures of American politics.

CONCLUSION:
THE MASS PUBLIC AND THE PRESIDENCY

It is impossible to know what the outcome of the 1936 election would have been had Roosevelt run a different campaign. The campaign he did run capitalized on the kinds of innovations and practices swirling around the country at the time. Roosevelt was not the only political actor to have access to polls, for example, which were beginning to be used by all campaigns as well as by the media. Roosevelt was not the only person to receive mail, although his correspondence was more extensive than most. He was not the only one to manage an organization or consider ways to mobilize his supporters, although his organization was more active and better funded than others. He was certainly not the only person speaking during 1936. The national airwaves were full of political arguments, from all points on the political compass, although no one else had quite his ability to convey warmth, reassurance, humor, and authority. The Roosevelt campaign, then, is not the only site where the changes discussed in this volume can be found, but it is a useful place through which we can observe and analyze them. That campaign, and the politics in which they were embedded, reveal important changes in our national political life.

The nation was large and diverse. As Roosevelt worked to expand the electorate to members of some groups, it was also important to manage that electorate. Polling was one way of capturing and distilling public opinion so that it could be made useful to campaigns and to the government. This process narrowed the ways in which the public could be understood by candidates and elected officials, however, and also reduced the range of expressions of opinion. Political parties, as large umbrella institutions, were unable to organize and mobilize the entire mass public, as the old party system reformed into the New Deal coalition. As Roosevelt reached across and remade party lines, he also relied on extrapartisan organizations to organize and mobilize support, which helped create his coalition and encouraged the view of national politics to be centered on a candidate rather than a party. He tried to manage the participation of the various members of his coalition, however. Emphasizing the idea that citizens of all educational levels were fully capable of comprehending and participating in politics, he treated those citizens as members of interest groups and offered them various degrees of welcome into national politics. Women were treated as both oriented toward the domestic and deeply entrenched in the civic. Members of organized labor unions were more gingerly mobilized, as their constitution as a collective always had the capacity to unsettle national stability. African Americans were symbolically treated as full members of the polity, but racial lines were strictly enforced. They were mobilized along those lines and were given few material benefits. In all these cases, inchoate groups of citizens were understood, organized, and mobilized according to their group affiliation. Those affiliations would become increasingly important valences in national politics.

The president and the presidency would also become more important, and this, more than any of the other changes associated with this election, is probably the direct result of the actions of Franklin D. Roosevelt rather than manifestations of changes and processes at work in the nation in the 1930s. Roosevelt offered the nation a vision of political security based on the protection of an empowered public by a strong national government. That government in turn was led by the president. Roosevelt wielded both partisan and extrapartisan organizations in his reelection campaign, and these organizations placed the candidate at the center of the campaign. He also placed the national government at the center of his vision for a more secure nation, arguing that only a truly national government could serve the nation as a whole. He placed the presidency at the center of that government, offering a vision of the nation that was united and protected by a strong leader. Importantly, that leader reflected the will of the people and was thus best understood as democratic rather than dictatorial. For Roosevelt, the presidency was a strong but democratic institution, authorized by the people to do its will. The bonds between the public and the president, then, empowered them both.

114   VOTING DELIBERATIVELY

This view of national politics marked a profound change in the practices of American politics, distilling government into the person of the president. These changes both granted citizens leverage over the system (to the extent that they were understood as members of groups able to pressure government) and removed them from it (to the extent that their opinions became reduced to polls and their preferences reduced to interests), affecting the ways the public deliberates in national elections and in politics as a whole.

Mastering Public Opinion, Silencing the Public

Franklin Roosevelt made superlative use of the emerging technologies available to him in 1936. Jim Farley's aide Emil Hurja, the Nate Silver of his day, worked not for the *New York Times* but for the president and his reelection campaign. The members of that campaign also began organizing early and kept organizing throughout the first term. Farley was in continual contact with party leaders around the nation, and Roosevelt himself maintained an extensive political correspondence. Through its appeal to the nation's clergy, the administration gave itself access to the thoughts and advice of many community leaders, reaching clergymen in large cities and small towns in every state. These efforts paid off for Roosevelt. He and his team out-organized, out-mobilized, and out-campaigned the opposition.

Out of the chaos that characterized politics in the 1930s, with vocal proponents of almost every political creed gaining adherents, Roosevelt was able to preside over a reasonably stable polity. In part, of course, this stability was the product of forces well beyond the president's control, such as national ideology and national mobility. He was able, however, to impart stability to the system by grounding his administration in public opinion. He had unparalleled access to the range of opinions floating around the nation. Supporters and opponents wrote him in unprecedented numbers. Aides such as Jim Farley maintained a voluminous correspondence, and Emil Hurja quantified opinions wherever possible. Roosevelt accessed political and religious community leaders, using that correspondence as a way of maintaining political support as well as tracking opinion. In all, then, the Roosevelt campaign had a wide, varied, and textured sense of the public and its opinions.

That sense, however, had to be condensed in order to be useful. Where FDR found both the time and the wherewithal to distill much of that opinion himself, later campaigns and later administrations would increasingly rely on flattened views and summary data. The public became reducible to demographics, regions, and demographics within regions. Their range of opinions became understood as "agree," "disagree," or "don't know." Both the public and its capacity to be heard by the government are diminished as their opinions are thus reduced. What began as an attempt to make public opinion available as a guide to public action has in practice reduced the public to usable data by a government rendered by its size and complexity increasingly immune to it.

Transcending Party, Emphasizing the Candidate

Roosevelt sought to remake the American political system. As part of that endeavor, he remade the American party system, altering previous lines of affiliation and the interests on which party affiliation was formed. He did this by changing the way the Democratic Party approached the election and by creating and relying on extrapartisan forms of political organization. Groups such as the Good Neighbor League and the Committee of One allowed citizens to participate in politics outside of partisan structures. Membership in such groups provided some of the interpersonal benefits of political participation and allowed group members to feel connected to their communities and able to contribute to them. They also provided something of a way station for those who had been Republicans and who might become Democrats. These groups were formed on the basis of shared principles and values and directed at the singular goal of reelecting the president.

The president, then, became the focus of the campaign and the focus on national politics. Those who participated in these extrapartisan organizations were encouraged to think of politics in terms of personality rather than platforms. Policies came to be associated with individuals rather than party. Roosevelt encouraged this understanding of politics, personally seeking and receiving an extraordinary commitment from the people to himself. Certainly, American politics has had charismatic and singularly important presidents before Roosevelt. But after his administration it would no longer be possible to govern as a party leader alone. The person of the president had become the dominant image in national politics, and national politics were increasingly understood through the presidency.

In some ways, this allows for greater access to the system. It is perhaps easier for the less politically informed to focus on a single condensation symbol. In other ways, it reduces both the understanding of and access to politics by ignoring the complexities of national policy making and by reducing the policy-making process to presidential governance. The system doesn't work the way we are encouraged to think it does, and the resulting ignorance and cynicism are not helpful to the long-term health of the political system as a whole. American governance often looks like but isn't, in reality, presidential governance.

Organizing the Electorate, Managing the System

Roosevelt understood the burgeoning power of interest groups in the American political context and sought to harness that power to his own ends. Under his administration the power of such groups expanded exponentially.[1] Women had considerably more influence within the government (at least in the departments and agencies devoted to social welfare and labor) and in the Democratic Party than is often realized, as the role of Molly Dewson so amply demonstrates. Labor came into its own, as a result of section 7(a) of the National Industrial Recovery Act and the Wagner Act, and became the Democratic Party's most reliable supporters.

Under the capable leadership of Dewson, in 1936 the DNC made explicit use of divisions dedicated to the organization of the mass public. It is notable that members of these groups were appreciated both as members of groups and also as members of a collective national enterprise. That is, the Roosevelt campaign appealed to them as women, as laborers, and, to a much lesser extent, as African Americans, whose particular vantage points and concerns were considered important, even integral, to the campaign. But they were, even in those individual manifestations, also understood as connected to a larger whole, composed of both the reelection effort and the entire nation. Group identity was treated as a subset of political identity, which was treated as a subset of national identity. In a complicated form of synecdoche, then, individual Roosevelt supporters could understand themselves as representing, for Roosevelt, the nation as a whole.

Roosevelt's campaign challenged inscribed hierarchies of gender, class, and race, not least by organizing women as "reporters" who pledged to learn about the issues and discuss them in small neighborhood enclaves. These women made use of all kinds of technology—the radio, newsletters, donkey banks, and local Interrogation Teas to inform and persuade voters and potential voters. Their work established women at the center of many of the New Deal's politics and policies. In all its campaign communication, the Roosevelt campaign treated voters as members of groups, neighborhoods, and communities and as individuals, important in their own right.

Members of those groups, however, were not all equally welcomed into the polity. While as citizens they were all treated as fully functioning intellects, capable of understanding complex questions and participating fully in politics, it is impossible not to also notice a certain degree of condescension in the election materials. Women were understood, for instance, to be primarily dedicated to domestic concerns, despite their capacities for political action. Members of labor unions were urged to support Roosevelt and to organize themselves toward his reelection, but the threat posed by such organization was understood and carefully managed. The utility of labor as an electoral army had always to be balanced by its threat as an industrial one. They were thus encouraged to believe that their economic self-interest was best served by loyalty to the political system and to its president. African Americans were treated with the greatest degree of condescension, and while they were symbolically welcomed into the polity, they were the group least encouraged to seek agency and most strongly encouraged to rely on representation. The limits of that representation were made obvious in the lack of civil rights legislation during the New Deal.

Roosevelt organized and mobilized his campaigns with a clear understanding of the geographic logic of the Electoral College. In doing so, he capitalized on the potential of subnational forms of political identity for motivating voters in a national election. His campaign treated those identities not as divisive but as profound sources of patriotism and national unity. The allegiances of wage workers, union members, and African Americans the Democrats fostered in 1936 have remained important elements of the Democrat's coalitional politics. Those politics, however, are also subject to fracturing and to being understood as less than the sum of its parts. The party can lose its sense of the common good in trying to fulfill the various needs and demands of its constituents understood primarily as members of groups.

Enacting the Will of the People Through a Single Institution

In 1936 Roosevelt ran on a specific and clearly articulated set of appeals: the need for a strong president at the head of an empowered national government as the surest means of protecting the nation's most vulnerable citizens from the depredations of those associated with the Republican Party; a national rather than a regional or local understanding of politics; and a consistent definition of his opponents as dedicated to self-interest rather than the national interest. Roosevelt benefited from the willingness of his opposition to fit into the definition he provided of them, and as a result the Republican Party seemed to render itself irrelevant in the short term and headed toward extinction over the longer term. At least in part because the American political system is designed in ways that protect and sustain two parties, and in part because of Roosevelt's second-term miscalculations, the Republican Party survived both in the 1930s and beyond. With its survival came also the continued survival of the issues and conflicts that characterized the 1936 election, almost all of which, as the 2012 election evidences, continue to structure our politics today.[2]

In 1936 the person of the president was at the center of the campaign. Roosevelt argued as if voters were reasoning and reasonable agents in their own right, citizens who made choices based on the national interest, not only on their own self-interest. The president promised to provide security for the nation as a whole and especially for its neediest citizens. Under FDR, the national government assumed responsibility for the well-being of its people. That responsibility meant an increase in both the size of government and the power of the executive branch. It also meant that the presidency assumed greater power and responsibility, which the constitutional design of the institution did not facilitate.

Presidents then look for other warrants for exercising power and find it in their ability to reflect, guide, and enact the "will of the people."[3] Perversely, that warrant, especially to the extent that it is grounded in the rather crude measure of public-opinion polls, is less often actually reflective of the general public and more reflective of other kinds of organizational needs. There is a huge tension between reflecting the organizational needs of managing a large governmental system and grounding that organization is some kind of discernible connection to public opinion. That is, however, the operative tension in the system Roosevelt bequeathed to us.

The Presidency and the Political System

Franklin D. Roosevelt is justly remembered for remaking the American political system. During his twelve years in office, Roosevelt reorganized the executive branch, rebalanced presidential relations with Congress and the Supreme

Court, and fundamentally altered the American party system and, with it, the contours of American political life.[4] He changed public expectations about the role of government.[5] He left us with a political system that depends on the president's personal relationship with the mass public, increasingly measured by and understood through public-opinion polls. That relationship developed during national campaigns, and it meant that managing those campaigns took on an importance beyond merely determining the next denizen of the Oval Office.[6] It is less often remembered that the bulk of this work was done in peacetime and in Roosevelt's first eight years.[7] In those years he established the federal government as the center of national political life and expanded the administrative bureaucracy.[8] He created the institution of the modern presidency.[9] Roosevelt changed the purpose of government as well as its size. Rather than serving the ends of a few, the national government under Roosevelt became, for the first time, an institution "directly experienced" by the vast majority of American citizens.[10] Not only did those citizens receive benefits from the national government, but millions also came to believe that the government, especially through its president, served them and their interests in ways never before attempted.[11] Roosevelt thus changed the relationship of the president to the people, marking that relationship with the indelible imprint of his own personality.[12] These changes began or were ratified in 1936.

The more important of these changes include the movement of power from states and localities to the national government, the vast increase in presidential authority that accompanied that change, the use of the federal administrative apparatus as a vehicle of governance, and the beginning of a shift from political parties as the organizing feature of campaigns and government to candidate-centered structures of power. In all these changes, there circle debates about the role of institutions and individuals, fears of propaganda and of demagoguery, and questions about the responsibilities of government in the lives of its citizens.

In exercising leadership in the way that he did, Roosevelt laid a trap for all his successors. That trap has been more or less consequential over time. Some presidents, most notably Ronald Reagan and Bill Clinton, have embraced the public role and its demands. Others, most notably George H. W. Bush and Barack Obama, have been less comfortable with that role. Given Obama's reputation for eloquence and his undeniable oratorical skill, it may seem odd to place him alongside the first Bush, but despite his public-speaking abilities, Obama has little love for politics and prefers administration.[13] Whatever else may be said about it, the contemporary presidency depends on an individual president's love of politics. The ability to treat voters as individuals, to connect with them across media, to impress on the electorate his (and I use that pronoun advisedly) personality, is crucial to any president's political success. It is also probably not enough to ensure that success.[14] Therein is the nature of the trap: Roosevelt understood public governance as part of the job, and he made it an integral element of the job. But he never confused the public performance with the entirety of his job, nor did he see it as anything more than one of a variety of ways to exert leverage over the system.

But because of his success and because of the structural changes that accompanied it, no president is free from Roosevelt's rhetorical and political legacies. The centrality of Social Security to the American political culture—and its hotly debated effects on the American political economy—continue. The election of 1936 was as much about the role of government in fostering a humane and human-centered view of politics as it was about anything else. The Progressives brought the issues of communal moral obligation onto the public agenda. Roosevelt, heir to that tradition, enacted those obligations into public policy on a scale the most ambitious Progressives could not have imagined and might not have approved of.[15] Those obligations were justified and continue to be justified in the policy debates that impel our national elections. Roosevelt's shadow lies over those elections as surely as it does over all the processes of governing in the United States.

Then and Now

The comparison of Roosevelt's 1936 campaign to our current politics has its limits as well, of course. First, Roosevelt had choices that candidates no longer have. It is true that the Democratic National Committee, especially the parts of it controlled by Molly Dewson, organized early and kept organizing. It is also true that this consistent organization helped foster support not only for the New Deal but also for the president's reelection effort. But that was a choice that reflected the kinds of choices available to Roosevelt. As this book is being completed, still within sight of the 2012 election, speculation is rife concerning the candidates for the 2016 contest, which remains years away. Some of those potential candidates have already been visiting early primary and caucus states, and many of them have formed exploratory committees and have started the arduous task of filling their campaign war chests. Roosevelt began organizing early. Contemporary candidates have no choice but to do so, and the definition of "early" had a very different meaning in 1936 than it does now.

In large part this necessity is driven by the need for money. When Molly Dewson and Jim Farley took a budget argument to FDR's office, the amount in question was less than $50,000, admittedly a significant sum in 1936.[16] But it pales in comparison to the contemporary context. Barack Obama's 2012 campaign cost over a billion dollars, and Mitt Romney raised nearly the same amount.[17] Most of the endless need for money comes from demands of retail politics—successful campaigns must reach individual citizens, and sometimes it seems they must strive to reach every single individual citizen. Candidates at all levels of politics are increasingly beholden to the process of securing money and to the donors who supply it. Roosevelt's need for money and the demands that fund-raising placed on him were so small by comparison as to be nonexistent.

Roosevelt relied on interest groups as constituent elements of his national campaign. His organization reached out to women, to minorities (at least in the North, where African Americans could legally vote), and to labor. Members of these groups and their leaders now give their allegiance to the parties on a fairly predictable basis, and they expect, as John L. Lewis expected, a return for that allegiance in terms of policy. Roosevelt was able and willing to resist the pressure members of such groups brought to bear on him and on his administration. Presidents and candidates now are considerably more likely to be understood—fairly or not—as captured by the demands of such groups.

The media environment has also changed. Roosevelt could assemble the entire Washington press corps in his office. He could also practically dictate coverage, and certain matters—such as his relationship with his wife and his private life in general—were considered out of bounds.[18] In the current context, we have footage of presidents in all manner of conditions and engaging in all manner of behavior. Their foibles and failings are all widely covered in the mainstream media. Moreover, technology has now broadened the access of ordinary citizens—the tape of Romney's famous "47 percent" remarks were made public over the Internet by a server at an event where those remarks were delivered and from which the media had been banned.[19] Roosevelt's campaign exercised considerable discipline and had substantial control over their mediated message. Such discipline is harder and harder to enforce, and such control is harder and harder to come by.

Roosevelt had the best of both worlds when it came to understanding public opinion. He and his aides at the DNC were pioneers in the new art and science of political polling. He also had access to a widely varied set of anecdotal forms of evidence for the state of national and local public opinion. He could calibrate those rich sources of opinion and derive from them a complicated and nuanced set of political appeals. Candidates in the current context rely almost exclusively on pollsters and the kinds of data at their disposal and nuance those data in very different ways. The public is understood and may be driven by appeals that seek to segment them. Roosevelt understood group affiliation as a single element in a complex calculus of political decision making. The current emphasis on "big data," on the one hand, seems to offer the promise of a complicated understanding of the interconnections among various political and other identities. On the other hand, reliance on these data also flattens the ways in which individuals can be understood. The stress on the common good, the experience of oneself as connected to the nation, may be lost in narrow appeals.

There is no doubt that governing in the present context is complicated. FDR governed at a time in which the electorate was narrowly understood. Large numbers of Americans were disenfranchised, and voter suppression was not only widely practiced, it was the constitutionally sanctioned law of the land. African Americans, migrant workers, and the poor in general were not polled and were often not encouraged or were actively prevented from voting, even in places where it was legal for them to do so. Presidential candidates today have to reach an infinitely more diverse electorate and have to find ways to accommodate that diversity. Roosevelt could—and did—ignore many people who now play much more important roles in campaigns. He had a more nuanced understanding of public opinion in a time when the public was much more restrictively understood.

All of which means that the question of political authority has altered a great deal since FDR's time—partly as a direct result of his actions. When Thomas Farrell noted that the Depression had affected the ways in which political authority was understood, he was absolutely right.[20] The nation's political and symbolic resources had been affected by the economic crisis. The economic crisis of 2012 also affected the national political and symbolic resources. Roosevelt was able to marshal new resources and revitalize old ones. It remains to be seen whether Obama and his successors can do the same.

NOTES

Archival Abbreviations

ALL	American Liberty League
DNC	Democratic National Committee
GNL	Good Neighbor League
GPF	General Political Files
LOC	Library of Congress
MDPC	Mary Dewson Pamphlet Collection
MPC	Miscellaneous Political Correspondence
OF	Official File
PPF	President's Personal File
RL	Franklin D. Roosevelt Presidential Library
WD	Women's Division

Introduction

 1. Leuchtenberg, *Franklin D. Roosevelt*; Leuchtenberg, *Shadow of FDR*.
 2. For an extended discussion of this point, see Hanson, *Democratic Imagination*, 255–77.
 3. The idea that elections are important moments in public deliberation has a long history. For the best recent work on the subject, see especially Delli Carpini, Cook, and Jacobs, "Public Deliberation," and Gastil, *By Popular Demand*.
 4. Atwill, "Rhetoric and Civic Virtue," 84.
 5. Ibid., 76.
 6. Beasley and Smith-Howell, "No Ordinary Rhetorical President," 7; Best, *Critical Press*, 11; Farrell, *Norms of Rhetorical Culture*; J. Flynn, *Roosevelt Myth*, 279; Gosnell, *Champion Campaigner*, 140; Hamby, *Survival of Democracy*, 122; Kennedy, *Freedom from Fear*, 137–38; Maney, *Roosevelt Presence*, 69–70; Parker, *Words That Reshaped America*; Ryan, *Roosevelt's Rhetorical Presidency*, 1.
 7. Arnold, *Making the Managerial Presidency*; Greer, *What Roosevelt Thought*, 91–93; Janeway, *Fall of the House*, 3.
 8. Lowi, *End of Liberalism*; see also Hofstadter, *Age of Reform*, 307, and McJimsey, *Presidency*, 85.
 9. Katznelson, *Fear Itself*, 478–79.
 10. See, especially, Green, *Eyes of the People*, and Lowi, *Personal President*.
 11. Tulis, *Rhetorical Presidency*.
 12. Alter, *Defining Moment*, 2.
 13. The evidence for this is both macro and micro. For a fascinating first-person account of life during the Depression, see Roth, *Great Depression*.

14. Venn, *New Deal*, 7.
15. Burner, *Herbert Hoover*, 310–17; A. Cohen, *Nothing to Fear*, 32; Smith, *FDR*, 282–87.
16. Roosevelt, "Inaugural Address," Mar. 4, 1933, in Rosenman, *Public Papers*, 2:11–16, 14. Rosenman edited thirteen volumes of papers and addresses; the first six were published in 1938 by Random House, the others by Macmillan in 1950.
17. A. Cohen, *Nothing to Fear*, 10; see also Schlesinger, *Age of Roosevelt*, 21.
18. Shesol, *Supreme Power*, 56.
19. On the weaknesses of the National Industrial Recovery Act, see A. Cohen, *Nothing to Fear*, 281–82; Kennedy, *Freedom from Fear*, 189; McElvaine, *Great Depression*, 160; McJimsey, *Presidency*, 72–73; and Schlesinger, *Age of Roosevelt*, 121. Despite these weaknesses, some considered the act important psychologically. See Greer, *What Roosevelt Thought*, 61, and Perkins, *The Roosevelt I Knew*, 277.
20. Brinkley, *Franklin Delano Roosevelt*, 39; Kennedy, *Freedom from Fear*, 183.
21. The *New York Times*, for instance, worried that the Economy Act would give the president "more arbitrary authority than any American statesman has had since the Constitution was framed." Quoted in A. Cohen, *Nothing to Fear*, 106.
22. The Civilian Conservation Corps remained one of the most popular of the New Deal programs. Badger, *FDR*, 57.
23. Leuchtenberg, *Franklin D. Roosevelt*, 123.
24. George McJimsey argues that the New Deal was best characterized as a triumph of "executive energy rapidly applied." *Presidency*, 36.
25. This strong association between the president and his program, of course, created both adulation and vehement opposition. On the latter, see J. Flynn, *Country Squire*, and Fried, *FDR and His Enemies*.
26. Roosevelt's method was the "new doctrine of presidential leadership" that Tulis refers to as one of the foundations of the rhetorical presidency. See Tulis, *Rhetorical Presidency*.
27. McElvaine, *Great Depression*, 286.
28. That "last word" was temporary, of course. After the election, the Court battle escalated. It ended with the "switch in time that saved nine," as Associate Justice Owen Roberts changed his position and voted to support New Deal legislation. Roosevelt declared victory; his program was safe. But the principle of judicial independence had also been affirmed, and the court-packing crisis had done considerable damage to the president. For details, see Shesol, *Supreme Power*.
29. Moley, quoted in introd. to Baskerville and Willett, *Nothing Else to Fear*, 4. The most recent critics of the New Deal include Shlaes, *Forgotten Man*; Folsom, *New Deal*; and Powell, *FDR's Folly*.
30. McElvaine, *Great Depression*, 116–18.
31. Best, *Critical Press*, 97; Leuchtenberg, *Franklin D. Roosevelt*, 73. For a defense of the Agricultural Adjustment Act, however, see Lippmann, "Agriculture," July 20, 1935.
32. See Farley, *Jim Farley's Story*, 46, and Schlesinger, *Age of Roosevelt*, 453. This episode was also the first time Roosevelt and Charles Lindbergh clashed. It would not be the last. See, among many others, Olson, *Those Angry Days*, xiv–xvi.
33. McElvaine, *Great Depression*, 251.
34. Shesol, *Supreme Power*, 107.
35. On Smith and the Liberty League, see Fried, *FDR and His Enemies*, 120–25.
36. Wolfskill and Hudson, *All But the People*, 163.
37. Krock, quoted in Shesol, *Supreme Power*, 111.
38. McElvaine, *Great Depression*, 238–40; for Coughlin, see Carpenter, "Father Charles E. Coughlin."

39. Hoover, quoted in Stephenson, *Campaigns and the Court*, 138–39.
40. See, for example, Lippmann's essay, "On Making Things," June 15, 1934. For a firsthand account of the accusations, see Ickes, *Secret Diary*, 683.
41. Shlaes, *Forgotten Man*, 265–66.
42. See White, *FDR and the Press*, 5. He had a more uneven relationship with columnists. See Best, *Critical Press*, 11.
43. Leuchtenberg, *Franklin D. Roosevelt*, 152.
44. Carlisle, *Hearst*, 166.
45. Shlaes, *Forgotten Man*, 251.
46. Wolfskill and Hudson, *All But the People*, 235.
47. For a contemporaneous understanding of the threat Long posed to the Roosevelt administration, see Lippmann, "Huey Long's Power," Mar. 7, 1935. On Long in general, see Badger, "Huey Long"; Iltis, "Demagoguery of Huey Long."
48. Unofficial Observer, *American Messiahs*, 9; Fried, *FDR and His Enemies*; McCoy, *Angry Voices*; Hogan and Williams, "Rusticity and Religiosity."
49. McJimsey, *Presidency*, 139.
50. Cashman, *America Ascendant*, 305.
51. Kennedy, *Freedom from Fear*, 218.
52. Fried, *FDR and His Enemies*, 63–64.
53. Charles Beard called the decline "staggering." McElvaine, *Great Depression*, 253.
54. *Time* called Roosevelt's election "the most overwhelming victory in the history of American politics." Quoted in McElvaine, *Great Depression*, 229.
55. Wolfskill and Hudson, *All But the People*, 219.
56. McElvaine, *Great Depression*, 257; Smith, *FDR*, 351.
57. King and Smith, *Still a House Divided*, 74.
58. Feinman, *Twilight of Progressivism*, 96.
59. Shlaes notes that prior to FDR, "liberal" had referred to policies connected to individualism; such policies were in turn associated with Republicans. Shlaes, *Forgotten Man*, 11.
60. See, for example, J. I. Hilliard, "Letter to the President," Sept. 18, 1934, OF 1150, ALL, Sept. 1934, RL; A. Gordon, "Letter to the President," Aug. 27, 1935, OF 1150, ALL, Aug. 1935, RL. Cartoonists and FDR supporters ridiculed the league as well. See, for example, J. W. Wiley, "Letter to the President" and attached political cartoon, Aug. 29, 1934, OF 1150, ALL, Aug. 1934, RL.
61. See correspondence between Hubert A. Smith and Louis Howe, Sept. 18, 1934, and attached resolutions. OF 1150, ALL, Sept. 1934, RL.
62. A number of people also wrote the White House condemning the president's attacks on the league. See, for instance, Victor K. McElheny, "Letter to the President," Sept. 6, 1934, OF 1150, ALL, Sept. 1934, RL. This letter is notable not least because the author attached a political cartoon in support of his views. Others felt the need to send the president copies of letters they wrote to the league, detailing the contributions made to them and the reasons for their actions and including newspaper articles or other evidence that the league's positions were correct on the issues. See, for instance, a letter with an illegible signature on stationery from McCracken County Property Owners Ass'n [sic], Jan. 20, 1936, OF 1150, ALL, 1936–37, RL.
63. See, for instance, the folder full of press releases, Liberty League Press Releases, 1935–36, box 34, RG 24, Harry L. Hopkins Papers, Federal Relief Agency Papers, RL. It is also interesting that a number of citizens felt the need to keep Roosevelt apprised of the league's activities. See Julius A. Bernstein, "Letter to the President," May 20, 1934, OF 1150, ALL, Sept. 1934, RL.

64. Schlesinger, *Age of Roosevelt*, 486–87.

65. So strong was this concern that Gallup included the following astounding question in its survey: "Do you believe that the acts and policies of the Roosevelt administration may lead to a dictatorship?" *Gallup Poll*, 30–31.

66. See Farley, *Behind the Ballots*, 293.

67. Smith, *FDR*, 362–63.

68. Weed, *Transformation*, 167, 180.

69. Lippmann, "The G.O.P., April 4, 1935," 275.

70. Leuchtenberg, *Franklin D. Roosevelt*, 175–77.

71. Gosnell, *Champion Campaigner*, 156. Among Republicans, Gallup reported that the top campaign issues were "governmental extravagance," "business regulation," "disregard of the Constitution," and "dictatorial government." *Gallup Poll*, 18.

72. Farley, *Jim Farley's Story*, 57.

73. Smith, *FDR*, 365.

74. For details on the convention, see Farley, *Behind the Ballots*, 293–308.

75. Jim Farley, for instance, divided the campaign into two phases: Roosevelt off the stump and Roosevelt on the stump. See *Behind the Ballots*, 309.

76. The details on Roosevelt's political trips are located in Trips of the President, OF 200HH, RL. His 1936 campaign trips are located in boxes 26–29, OF 200HH, RL.

77. Roosevelt, "Campaign Address at Madison Square Garden," Oct. 31, 1936, in Rosenman, *Public Papers*, 5:566–73.

78. Gosnell, *Champion Campaigner*, 164.

79. These were the main arguments Landon made against Social Security. See "Promise the Moon."

80. Gallup, *Gallup Poll*, 35.

81. Gosnell, *Champion Campaigner*, 166.

82. Webber, *New Deal Fat Cats*, 127.

83. Robinson, *They Voted for Roosevelt*, 28.

84. Leuchtenberg, *Franklin D. Roosevelt*, 185.

85. The Republicans spent $8.8 million; the Democrats spent $5.1 million. Webber, *New Deal Fat Cats*, 7.

86. See Holli, *Wizard of Washington*, 44.

87. On Hurja's polling prior to the 1936 election, see Weed, *Transformation*, 161.

88. Holli, *Wizard of Washington*, 58–59. Certainly, in Hurja's capacity at the Democratic National Committee and as aide to Jim Farley, he maintained extensive files on patronage. They comprise boxes 90–96 of his papers and fill boxes of his political correspondence as well. See the Emil Hurja Collection, RL.

89. Smith, *FDR*, 374.

90. One Roosevelt critic goes so far as to declare the creation of "a new kind of interest group politics" the reason for his victory in 1936. Shlaes, *Forgotten Man*, 10–11. See also Badger, *FDR*, 81.

91. Milkis, *President and the Parties*, 64–66.

Chapter 1

1. Susan Herbst, for instance, identifies 1936 as a pivotal year in her history of public opinion. See *Numbered Voices*. According to J. Michael Hogan, George Gallup also identified 1936 as the "starting point of the modern era in polling." See "George Gallup," 163.

2. Numerous scholars have addressed the ways in which public opinion understood through polls proves detrimental to public deliberation. See, for example, Hauser, "Vernacular Dialogue"; Hauser and Benoit-Barne, "Reflections on Rhetoric"; Herbst, *Numbered Voices*; Hogan et al., "National Task Force"; and Smith and Hogan, "Public Opinion."

3. Maney, *Roosevelt Presence*, 71. Anthony J. Badger puts the number at "more than six thousand" a day and notes that in the week after the first inaugural, 460,000 letters arrived at the White House. *FDR*, xi. The public also responded to specific speeches, policies, and events. The PPF 200 files, where these responses are kept, fill 304 boxes. There are also letters, including those addressed to Eleanor Roosevelt, in other collections. It is impossible to determine precisely the number of letters the White House received, but a conservative estimate of 5,000 a day over the course of the administration provides a total of 13 million letters, a number that seemed reasonable to the archivists at the Roosevelt Library.

4. Significant disparity exists among estimates of how many clergy actually replied, although the best estimates seem to be somewhere between seven thousand and nine thousand. The Roosevelt Library collection of letters and supporting documents, the PPF 21A files, fills thirty-five boxes.

5. Herbst, *Numbered Voices*, 165.

6. Hogan et al., "National Task Force."

7. Tulis, *Rhetorical Presidency*.

8. But see Milkis, *Theodore Roosevelt*.

9. For a history of public-opinion polling and the presidency, see Eisinger, *Evolution of Presidential Polling*.

10. Ibid., 14. See also Hogan, "George Gallup."

11. Holli, *Wizard of Washington*, 46.

12. I make this argument at length in Stuckey, *Good Neighbor*.

13. Editor of *Collier's*, quoted in Best, *Critical Press*, 15.

14. The relationships between members of the Roosevelt administration and the politicians of Tammany Hall are fascinating, if beyond the scope of this book. Roosevelt himself had a very tricky relationship with the Tammany machine; Farley tended to be on the outside, wanting in; others, like Frances Perkins, maintained close relationships with Tammany politicians. On Roosevelt and Tammany, see Smith, *FDR*, 70–78; on Farley and Tammany, see Scroop, *Mr. Democrat*, 21–22, 133; on Perkins and Tammany, see Downey, *Woman Behind the New Deal*, 37–39.

15. Eisinger, *Evolution of Presidential Polling*, 82.

16. Robert Rhea, "Letter to James A. Farley," Jan. 14, 1936, Registration and Statistical Data, 1936, GPF, box 81, Hurja Papers (unarranged), RL.

17. Farley, *Jim Farley's Story*, 35.

18. Milkis, *Political Parties*, 7, 76–77. See also Milkis, "Introduction," 16. On FDR and the administrative state, see Arnold, *Making the Managerial Presidency*, 81–114, and Walcott and Hult, *Governing the White House*.

19. Burns, *Roosevelt*, 276.

20. Farley, *Behind the Ballots*, 308.

21. See copies of correspondence in "OF 300, Farley's Corres, General July 30–Aug 31, 1936" and "OF 300, Farley's Corres, General, Sept. 1–21, 1936," both found in OF 300, box 35, DNC, RL. Many of these letters were forwarded to Roosevelt.

22. Farley lost no time in forwarding this letter to both Roosevelt and the First Lady. See copies of correspondence in "Farley's Corres, General July 30–Aug 31, 1936."

23. V. J. Dollman to James A. Farley, Sept. 9, 1936, "OF 300, Farley's Corres, General, Sept. 1–21, 1936."

24. Letter to James A. Farley, no author, n.d., "Farley's Corres, General July 30–Aug 31, 1936."

25. Not all this correspondence was helpful, although some of it was entertaining. C. U. Galbraith, for instance, wrote Hurja concerning the "well-known fact in Hollywood" that William Randolph Hearst had murdered Thomas H. Ince, his rival for the affections of an unnamed "prominent motion picture star." Mr. Galbraith also offered to put his expertise as a filmmaker at the disposal of the Roosevelt campaign. C. U. Galbraith, "Letter to Emil Hurja," Oct. 6, 1936, Emil Hurja, "Miscellaneous Political Correspondence Requiring Dictated Reply," 1936–37, folder 1, box 62, Hurja Papers, RL.

26. Stephen Early, "Memo to Jim Farley," July 30, 1936, "Farley's Corres, General July 30–Aug 31, 1936."

27. Farley later wrote, "a political leader's first responsibility is to get his party elected." "The New Breed of Politician," undated manuscript, box 71, James A. Farley Papers, LOC, Washington, D.C.

28. Patronage became a critical focal point for both Farley's power and challenges to it, a fact underlined most clearly in his relationship with Molly Dewson. Scroop, *Mr. Democrat*, 107–12. See also Dewson, "An Aid to the End," Campaign Materials, box 26, Dewson Papers, RL, 1:40–44, 124; 2:25–38, 181–85.

29. Burns, *Roosevelt*, 278. For an example of such criticism directed at the president instead of at Farley, see J. Flynn, *Country Squire*, 90–96.

30. For a discussion of Progressivism and the New Deal, see Keller, "Progressivism," 313–22; Feinman, *Twilight of Progressivism*.

31. See, for example, "Big Jim Farley: He Gets the Blame," *Saturday Evening Post*, June 27, 1936, 5, 93. On the ways in which the reformist impulse combined with corporatism and planning, see Ira Katznelson's discussion of the NIRA in *Fear Itself*, 231; on the ways in which that impulse clashed with New Deal politics, see Scroop, *Mr. Democrat*.

32. Smith, *FDR*, 370.

33. See the material found in "Long, Huey, Printed Matter," box 52, Farley Papers, LOC.

34. Farley, *Behind the Ballots*, 249–50.

35. Burns, *Roosevelt*, 287; Farley, *Behind the Ballots*, 314.

36. Jackson, *That Man*, 20.

37. Memo from James A. Farley to the president, Nov. 2, 1936, "Presidential Campaign, 1936, Campaign Book, (1)," Farley Papers, LOC.

38. Scroop, *Mr. Democrat*, 131.

39. In June 1947 Farley wrote a five-part series for *Collier's*, titled "Why I Broke with Roosevelt," detailing the president's duplicity in various matters and specifically concerning the third term. Box 71, Farley Papers, LOC.

40. Scroop, *Mr. Democrat*, 2.

41. Milkis and Mileur note, for example, that the New Deal realignment was the first to put the executive rather than the party at the heart of the program. See their introduction to *Triumph of Liberalism*, 8. See also Milkis, *Political Parties*, 99.

42. Franklin D. Roosevelt, "Sample Form Letter," PPF 21 (X-Refs), 21A (AL-AZ), "PPF 21A Clergy Letters Sample Form Letter," box 2, RL.

43. See, for example, Hugh Gary, "Letter to the President," Sept. 28, 1935, Clergy Letters, Colo., and Duncan S. Merwin, "Letter to the President," Oct. 7, 1935, Clergy Letters, Calif., both in PPF 21A (CA-CT), box 5, RL. Hereafter all letters are cited by author, date, location, and box number.

44. Hauser, *Vernacular Voices*, 264.

45. Howard A. Gibbs, for example, sent a photo of the children attending his Bible school. Howard A. Gibbs, n.d., Fort Defiance, Ariz., box 2.

46. See, for example, Ralph Supplee, Oct. 18, 1935, box 11, Dunkerton, Iowa, and Edward A. Durham, Oct. 10, 1935, Claremont, N.H., box 19.

47. Hauser treats these letters as examples of the vernacular rhetoric he considers critical to democracy. See *Vernacular Voices*, 28–33.

48. Roosevelt, however, did reference one letter in his famous Quarantine Address.

49. These data are all reported in "Report on Clergy Letters," n.d., "Public Papers and Addresses: Memos to Be Used for Annotation: China and Japan, Transportation of Munitions to–Cotton," box 34, Samuel I. Rosenman Papers, RL, 1–4.

50. See letter from Sam Rosenman to Stephen Early, Sept. 1, 1937, ibid. A copy of FDR's letter to the clergy is one of the very few letters to appear in the published *Public Papers*. See Franklin D. Roosevelt, "The President Asks for the Counsel and Help of the Clergy of America," in Rosenman, *Public Papers*, 4:370.

51. "Report on Clergy Letters," 5.

52. Theodore Bauer, Oct. 24, 1935, Des Moines, Iowa, box 11.

53. Lorenz I. Harrison, Nov. 7, 1935, Andover, Mass., box 15.

54. For a good discussion of the role and consequences of the New Deal's emphasis on planning, see McJimsey, *Presidency*, 65–66. For a discussion of how that applied to farming, see Kennedy, *Freedom from Fear*, 140.

55. In January 1936, 59 percent of Americans polled opposed the Agricultural Adjustment Act. Best, *Critical Press*, 97.

56. Don M. Chase, Oct. 10, 1935, San Francisco, Calif., box 4.

57. On the National Recovery Administration and its failures, see Kennedy, *Freedom from Fear*, 183–89; McJimsey, *Presidency*, 72–73; and Venn, *New Deal*, 42.

58. Wolfskill and Hudson, *All But the People*, 183.

59. Gould, *Modern American Presidency*, 93.

60. Wolfskill and Hudson, *All But the People*, 183.

61. A. N. Lindsay, Nov. 14, 1935, Clinton, Mo., box 18.

62. Lim, *Anti-Intellectual Presidency*.

63. Maverick, quoted in Schlesinger, *Age of Roosevelt*, 360.

64. D. W. Hawkins, Sept. 25, 1935, Andulasia, Ala., box 2. Similar sentiments were expressed by J. W. Fitzgerald, Sept. 7, 1935, illegible city, N.C., box 23.

65. Robert C. Rhodes, Oct. 23, 1935, Emory University, Ga., box 7.

66. Roosevelt and his aides generally shared this concern. Harry Hopkins, for instance, noted that "work is a moral habit in America." Hopkins, "Federal Relief," Sept. 19, 1936, 87.

67. "Report on Clergy Letters," 17; Wolfskill and Hudson, *All But the People*, 179.

68. It was indeed an important program both in terms of the people it helped and the political benefits of such help: estimates are that roughly 80 percent of Works Progress Administration workers voted the Democratic ticket. McJimsey, *Presidency*, 103.

69. On the strengths and weaknesses of this legislation, see McElvaine, *Great Depression*, 257.

70. William Grant Smith, Oct. 21, 1935, Delphi, Ind., box 10.

71. James W. Hailwood, Oct. 14, 1935, Grand Rapids, Mich., box 16.

72. Lawrence Radcliffe, Oct. 1, 1935, Daytona Beach, Fla., box 5. See also O. M. Showalter, Sept. 26, 1935, Emporia, Kans., box 12. The Townsend Plan, often considered an influence on Social Security, was premised on the idea of giving citizens over a certain age a monthly stipend on the condition that they did not work and spent the money immediately, providing jobs for younger citizens and fueling the economy. For more on the plan, see "Townsend Plan Movement."

73. Little help for people of color would be forthcoming. See Zinn, *People's History*, 394–96, for a discussion of African Americans and the New Deal in 1935–36. Still, African

Americans strongly supported Roosevelt and the New Deal, especially after 1936. Nancy J. Weiss notes that 1936 "brought black Americans decisively into the Roosevelt coalition." See *Farewell*, 180.

74. Glenn B. Coyenkill, Oct. 23, 1935, N.Y., box 1.

75. On New Deal programs and American Indians, see Philp, *Indian Self-Rule*, and Takaki, *Different Mirror*, 238–44.

76. Samuel James Grier, Oct. 22, 1935, Arkadelphia, Ark., box 3.

77. For an extended discussion of the pleas for national help, see Katznelson, *Fear Itself*.

78. Jesse Tidball, Oct. 22, 1935, Madison, Ind., box 10; R. J. Lorance, Oct. 16, 1935, Auburn, Neb., box 19.

79. Fred O. Brose, Nov. 12, 1935, box 8, Rupert, Idaho. Similar sentiments were expressed by George W. Bell, Sept. 28, 1935, Whiteville, Tenn., box 30.

80. McJimsey, *Presidency*, 108. On the political and cultural dynamics of women's work during the Depression, see Kessler-Harris, *In Pursuit of Equity*, 64–116, and Kessler-Harris, *Out to Work*, 250–71.

81. George H. Schuster, Nov. 11, 1935, Ingelwood, Calif., box 5.

82. R. D. Robeson, n.d., Springfield, Ohio, box 23.

83. Hurja, quoted in Holli, *Wizard of Washington*, 68.

84. Emil Hurja, "Miscellaneous Political Correspondence Requiring No Reply or Form Letter," 1936–37, folder 3, box 63, Hurja Papers, RL.

85. See the election forecasts found in OF 300, box 40, DNC, RL; "Speech Material: Public Opinion Polls" and various newspaper clippings found in "Speech Material: National Debt and Budget; Public Utilities," PPF 1820, box 13, RL.

86. Gallup, of course, would go on to wield important influence in future administrations. See Hogan, "Cold War Strategy," 134–68.

87. For a similar take on the use of these new techniques, see Milkis, "Franklin D. Roosevelt," 57.

88. Susan Herbst makes this argument in detail. See *Numbered Voices*.

89. Krock, quoted in Weed, *Transformation*, 179.

90. See, for example, Emil Hurja, Registration and Statistical Data, 1936, GPF, Hurja Papers, box 81, RL; Emil Hurja, folder 1, National Inquirer Poll, Statistical Raw Files, 1936, GPF, box 74, Hurja Papers, RL.

91. See folder labeled "Poll Data," in Emil Hurja, GPF, Statistical Analysis: Registration Data, 1936, box 81, RL.

92. "Letter from National Campaign Committee to Secy's of State," Oct. 12, 1936, "Miscellaneous Political Correspondence, Oct. 1936," MPC, 1935–37, box 61, Hurja Papers, RL.

93. Weed, *Transformation*, 161. Hoover did not deserve all the criticism heaped on him. For good discussions of the Hoover presidency, see Burner, *Herbert Hoover*; Fausold, *Presidency*; and Wilson, *Herbert Hoover*.

94. Emil Hurja, "Registration Data," Statistical Analysis: Registration Data, 1936, GPF, box 81, Hurja Papers, RL.

95. Emil Hurja, folder 3, National Inquirer Poll, Statistical Raw Files, 1936, GPF, box 74, Hurja Papers, RL.

96. "Pres Campaign 1936, State Reports" (Hurja Papers), box 56, Farley Papers, LOC.

97. "Memo to Mrs. Godwin," Oct. 16, 1936, "Hurja, Emil: Gen Corres," box 90, RG 24, General Correspondence 1933–40, Hu-Hyde Park Conference, Sept. 1935, box 90, Hopkins Papers, RL.

98. The White House kept its eye on many of those polls. See, for example, the information on *Literary Digest* polls maintained in the West Wing: "Public Opinion Polls: 1935–41,"

President's Secretary's File, "Post War thru Railroads: General," box 157, President's Subject File, RL. Citizens also shared polling data with the president. See W. L. Hotchkiss, "Letter to the President," May 7, 1935, "Speech Material: Public Opinion Polls" and "Speech Material: National Debt," PPF 1820, RL.

99. Emil Hurja, folder 3, National Inquirer Poll, Statistical Raw Files, 1936, GPF, box 74, Hurja Papers, RL. Scholars have noted the impact congressional voting had on patronage. Eisinger, *Evolution of Presidential Polling*, 83.

100. See, for example, the wealth of material in "Speech Material: National Politics," PPF 1820 and "Speech Material: National Debt," PPF 1820, RL. See also a report on responses to the New Deal program, sent to Eleanor Roosevelt, and consisting primarily of data culled for personal interviews and detailing reactions from farmers, industrial workers, and members of the business community, broken down by region. George Allen, "Letter to Eleanor Roosevelt," July 7, 1935, "Speech Material: Public Opinion Polls" and "Speech Material: National Debt," PPF 1820, RL.

101. Burns, *Roosevelt*, 282.

102. Milkis, "Franklin D. Roosevelt," 34, 47. He locates many of the reasons for party decline in the practices of the New Deal. See Milkis, *President and the Parties*.

103. Landy, "Presidential Party Leadership," 73.

104. Milkis, *Political Parties*, 3.

Chapter 2

1. Farley, *Jim Farley's Story*, 59.
2. There are, of course, also problems with strictly procedural definitions of democracy. See Hauser and Benoit-Barne, "Reflections on Rhetoric," 265–66.
3. See, for instance, Kock and Villasden, *Rhetorical Citizenship*; Skocpol, *Diminished Democracy*; and Young, *Inclusion and Democracy*.
4. This is the kind of grounded work in citizenship done most prominently in rhetoric by Robert Asen. See, for instance, his "Normative Conception" and "Discourse Theory"; see also Waisanen, "Robust Public Engagement."
5. Milkis, *Political Parties*, 2.
6. Jeff Shesol argues, however, that the Liberty League wanted to co-opt the Republican Party. See *Supreme Power*, 162.
7. See Stuckey, "Great Debate," 8.
8. Burnham, *Critical Elections*. Note, however, the challenges to realignment theory, such as Shafer, *End of Realignment*.
9. Kennedy, *Freedom from Fear*, 216.
10. On the significance of these new groups to the national electorate, see Polenberg, *Era*, 133.
11. See the correspondence between Farley and FDR, "Roosevelt, Franklin D., 1934," box 34, Farley Papers, LOC.
12. George McJimsey notes the importance of this in FDR's thinking. See *Presidency*, 87.
13. At least one scholar sees the New Deal as both a link to and subversion of Progressive values. See Eisenach, *Sacred Discourse*, chap. 5.
14. Milkis, *Political Parties*, 76.
15. Wolfskill and Hudson, *All But the People*, 61.
16. Many of these trends were made clear in the report issued by the United States President's Committee on Social Trends, completed by many of the nation's best social scientists

and commissioned by Hoover. Drafts of the report can be found in United States President's Committee on Social Trends Papers, box 16, LOC.

17. For a discussion of the threats to that stability, see Zinn, *People's History*, 384–99.

18. Shogan, *Prelude to Catastrophe*, 10.

19. Kanawada, *Roosevelt's Diplomacy*, 21.

20. One way FDR reconciled those interests was by mobilizing John A. Ryan on his behalf, so Coughlin's voice was not the only one heard by Catholics. For details on Ryan's rhetoric and his activities in 1936, see Medhurst, "Argument and Role."

21. On "the Klan impulse," see Hofstadter, *Age of Reform*, 293–94. On the disproportionate suffering of African Americans, see, among many others, McElvaine, *Great Depression*, 187–93.

22. For a discussion of the low salience of race among New Dealers, see Weiss, *Farewell*, 37–39; McMahon, *Reconsidering Roosevelt*, 29; and Wolfskill and Hudson, *All But the People*, 89.

23. Brinkley, *Unfinished Nation*, 701–2.

24. See Bunche, *Political Status*, 83–94.

25. Hofstadter, *Age of Reform*, 298–301.

26. Greer, *What Roosevelt Thought*, 19.

27. Janeway, *Fall of the House*, 30.

28. Wolfskill and Hudson, *All But the People*, 119.

29. On FDR's penchant for the middle ground, see Dalleck, *Hail to the Chief*, 94.

30. McElvaine, *Great Depression*, 254.

31. Louise Lazell, "Letter to Governor John C. Winant," Oct. 1, 1936, "Social Security Board, Speaking Engagements in Defense of Social Security," "Smith Geoffrey, 1935–37," John Winant Papers, 1935–Feb. 1941, box 165, RL.

32. Charles Stelzle, "The Good Neighbor League: Its Program and Its Possibilities," n.d., Correspondence File, GNL Campaigns and Programs, GNL Papers, RL, 1.

33. "The Good Neighbor League, Inc: Its Principles, Purpose, Program, and Activities," n.d., Correspondence File, GNL Campaigns and Programs, GNL Papers, RL, 3.

34. "Aims and Purposes of the Good Neighbor League," memo, n.d., Correspondence File, GNL Campaigns and Programs, Objectives and Purposes, 1937–38, "General Organization Barr, Louis D.," box 8, GNL Papers, RL.

35. A similar tactic was used in the development of the Committee of One appeals. See Vertical File: Campaign Literature, 1936, Committee of One for the Re-election of President Roosevelt, RL.

36. Herbert Gaston, "Letter to Henry," with cover memo from Mrs. Morgenthau to Miss Dewson, Aug. 22, 1936, "Folder #10, Dem Nat'l Comm, Women's Div–Corresp–General, Good Neighbor League, 1936," DNC, WD, 1933–44, General Correspondence 1933–37, Form Letters, 1930–32, Department of the Interior, 1933–36, box 5, RL.

37. Stelzle, "Good Neighbor League," 1.

38. "Program of the Good Neighbor League for the Year 1937," n.d., Correspondence File, GNL Campaigns and Programs, Objectives and Purposes, 1937–38, General Organization, Louis D. Barr, GNL Campaigns and Programs, Objectives and Purpose of GNL, box 8, GNL Papers, RL.

39. See "Report from Louis Barr," Aug. 12, 1936, Newark, New Jersey, Organizational Meeting, Correspondence File, General Organization, Louis D. Barr, GNL Campaigns and Programs, Objectives and Purpose of GNL, box 8, GNL Papers, RL.

40. *Don't You Want This Kind of an America*, pamphlet, Good Neighbor League, "Franklin, Benjamin-Gram, Hans," Eleanor Roosevelt Pamphlet Collection, RL.

41. Lazell, "Governor John C. Winant."
42. For an example of the former, see Howard A. Wilson, "Letter to Mr. McIntyre," June 24, 1935; for an example of the latter, see Eleanor Mae Gregor, "Letter to the President," June 22, 1935, both in "PPF 200B, Public Reaction, June 19, 1935," PPF 200B, April 28, 1935, L–Z, 6/19.35, box 21, RL.
43. Wolfskill and Hudson, *All But the People*, 61–62.
44. McElvaine, *Great Depression*, 177–79.
45. Hopkins, "Federal Relief," 87.
46. Schlesinger, *Age of Roosevelt*, 476.
47. Bennett Champ Clark, "Letter," May 23, 1936, "Committee of One Miscellaneous Correspondence," Committee of One, Correspondence, Lists, Publications, GPF, box 86, Hurja Papers, RL.
48. James A. Farley, "Letter," Aug. 24, 1936, "Committee of One Miscellaneous Correspondence," Hurja Papers, RL.
49. Ibid.
50. Farley, "Letter," n.d., "Committee of One Miscellaneous Correspondence," Hurja Papers, RL.
51. Clark, "Letter," n.d., Vertical File: Campaign Literature, 1936, Committee of One for the Re-election of President Roosevelt, RL.
52. Material all found in Vertical File: Campaign Literature, 1936, Committee of One for the Re-election of President Roosevelt, RL.
53. Clark, "Letter to Fellow Member," n.d., "Committee of One Miscellaneous Correspondence," Hurja Papers, RL.
54. Clark, "Letter," Aug. 7, 1936, "Committee of One Miscellaneous Correspondence," Hurja Papers, RL.
55. Western Union to Edward C. Johnston, Oct. 5, 1936, Vertical File, Campaign Literature, 1936, Committee of One for the Re-election of President Roosevelt, RL.
56. Emil Hurja, "Memo to Mr. Farley," Nov. 1, 1936, Committee of One, Records and Papers, 1936, GPF, box 85, Hurja Papers, RL.
57. "Important Notice: Special Instructions to Members of Committee of One," Committee of One, Records and Papers, GPF, box 85, Hurja Papers, RL.
58. Ibid.
59. Ibid.
60. Emil Hurja, *What About the National Debt*, Committee of One, Records and Papers, GPF, box 85, Hurja Papers, RL, 1. This flyer was produced by the Roosevelt All-Party Agricultural Committee, an association like the CO; I mix the two here because the purposes and theory behind them are the same.
61. Ibid., 2.
62. Ibid., 3.
63. Hurja, "Memo to Mr. Farley." There is a letter from Clark asking members to help finance a special radio talk by the president for members of the CO. See Clark, "Letter," Aug. 22, 1936, Committee of One Miscellaneous Correspondence," Hurja Papers, RL.
64. A. Cohen, *Nothing to Fear*, 285.
65. Brinkley, *Unfinished Nation*, 696.
66. Downey, *Woman Behind the New Deal*, 344.
67. Shlaes, *Forgotten Man*, 299.
68. Carlisle, *Hearst*, 177.
69. Alter, *Defining Moment*, xv; Milkis, "Franklin D. Roosevelt," 33.
70. See Stuckey, *Good Neighbor*.

Chapter 3

1. Young, *Inclusion and Democracy*.
2. Shlaes, *Forgotten Man*, 10–11. See also Badger, *FDR*, 81.
3. Eisinger, *Evolution of Presidential Polling*, 11.
4. McJimsey, *Presidency*, 85. See also Leuchtenberg, *Franklin D. Roosevelt*, 84.
5. Milkis, *President and the Parties*, 64–66.
6. Eleanor, in fact, proposed Dewson as head of "a kind of Democratic Women's Council" in September 1935. See Eleanor's correspondence to Farley, "Roosevelt, Eleanor, 1932–36," box 34, Farley Papers, LOC.
7. On women's work and the ways that work was affected by the Depression, see Kessler-Harris, *Out to Work*, 249–71.
8. On the ways in which the New Deal and New Deal politics were gendered—and raced within those gender dynamics—see, most prominently, Kessler-Harris, *In Pursuit of Equity*, 64–116. On the ways in which the Depression encouraged traditional views of "women's place," see Brinkley, *Unfinished Nation*, 661.
9. Kessler-Harris, *Out to Work*, 251. Susan Ware notes that in 1936, four-fifths of those questioned thought that married women should have jobs. See *Beyond Suffrage*, 2. Married women workers, it should be noted, remained in the minority, even among very low-income families. See Wandersee, *Women's Work*, 2.
10. Ware, *Partner and I*, 89–91. In the 1980s there was a burst of interest in women between 1920 and 1960, but the period does seem to have received relatively little attention; however, see Scharf and Jensen, *Decades of Discontent*.
11. Zinn writes dismissively, "There was no great feminist movement in the thirties. But many women became involved in the labor organizing of those years." *People's History*, 396. For a similar take, see Brinkley, *Unfinished Nation*, 662.
12. Ware, *Beyond Suffrage*, 1.
13. Of Roosevelt, Dewson noted in her (unpublished) autobiography that she "always had his thorough-going support." She also states that if she ever had trouble getting access to the president, all she had to do was ask for help from the First Lady. See "Aid to the End," box 26, Dewson Papers, RL, 1:1, 2.
14. For a detailed discussion of Dewson's political and personal life, see Ware, *Partner and I*.
15. Ibid., 200.
16. Mileur, "The Boss," 114–15; McJimsey, *Presidency*, 149. See also "Democratic National Convention, 1936," box 7, Dewson Papers, DNC, 1936, RL; *Democratic Digest*, 1937, Correspondence with State Leaders, Subject Files, DNC-Lists, Dewson Western Trip, box 7, WD, DNC, Dewson Papers, RL.
17. See "Scrapbook, Politics, Western Trip, 1936," 1936 Campaign, Politics, box 23, Dewson Papers, RL.
18. On her activity in party affairs, see Mary W. Dewson, "Memo to W. Forbes Morgan," Jan. 17, 1936, "Democratic National Convention, 1936," and *Democratic Digest*, 1927, box 7, Dewson Papers, DNC, 1936; RL. On her work for women's patronage, see the correspondence in Social Security Board, 1933–36, School Teachers, 1936, General Correspondence, 1933–37, Women's International League for Peace and Freedom, 1935–36, box 11, WD, DNC, 1933–44, RL.
19. She tracked representation by state. See her map, "Dewson Papers, Campaign of 1936–Program Matters," Correspondence with State Lead Constitutional Amendment, Committee on Economic Security, Civil Service, Child Labor Amendment, Campaign of 1936, Subject Files, box 8, Dewson Papers, RL.

20. Mary W. Dewson, "To the Women Democratic Leaders," n.d., Speeches and Articles, 1936, box 9, Dewson Papers, RL.
21. Ibid.
22. Mary W. Dewson, "Democratic Visitors, Get Inside That Door!" "Dewson Papers, Campaign of 1936–Articles, Drafts, Corresp," Buenos Aires Conference, Campaign of 1936, Subject Files, box 5, Dewson Papers, RL.
23. "Scrapbook," Dewson Papers, RL.
24. For example, she provided flow charts recommending the duties of staff members and clarifying where each staff position fit in the hierarchy. *The Favored State Party Set-Up for Democratic Women*, MDPC, 1–12, box 1, WD, DNC, RL.
25. Dewson, quoted in Ware, *Partner and I*, 196.
26. This strategy was among those in which Dewson owed a debt to the suffrage experience and what women learned from it. In her files, for instance, there are copies of pamphlets by Nancy Hale, titled *What the Women Could and Should Do for the Democratic Party* and *What Interests Women and Why*. Dewson wrote a note on the cover, which reads, "This analysis of Nancy Hale agrees with my ideas on which I based my Reporter Plan (1932) and all my political plans. M. W. Dewson, 1936," MDPC, 30–40, box 3, RL.
27. *The "A-B-C" of a Successful Election*, MDPC, 1–12, RL.
28. *The Precinct Campaign School for Democratic Women*, MDPC, 1–12, RL.
29. See Rainbow Fliers, 1936, Form Letters, 1940, Campaign Material, General Correspondence, 1937–44, WD, DNC, 1933–44, RL.
30. These fliers made their first appearance in 1930; they owe a great deal to the practices of the suffragettes. See Ware, *Partner and I*, 161.
31. Rainbow Fliers, WD, DNC, RL.
32. Rainbow Fliers were spectacularly popular. See the testimonials to that effect: Rainbow Fliers, WD, DNC, RL.
33. Dewson, "Aid to the End," box 27, Dewson Papers, RL, 2:2.
34. Mary W. Dewson, "Letter," Oct. 16, 1936, Buenos Aires Conference, Dewson Papers, RL.
35. The Roosevelt record on race is unimpressive, to say the least. Nonetheless, African Americans became an important element in the New Deal coalition. See Weiss, *Farewell*, 180.
36. Mary W. Dewson, *You, Mrs. County Leader, are the Keystone in the Arch of Democratic Victory*," Dem Nat'l Comm, Women's Div—General Corresp—Campaign Material; Democratic National Committee, Women's Division 1933–1944, General Correspondence 1937–1944, Campaign material—"Rainbow Fliers"—1936—Form Letters 1940, RL. Initially, ten thousand copies were printed. Dewson noted with pride that "ultimately, a million were struck off on order." See Scrapbook, in "Aid to the End," box 26, Dewson Papers, RL, 1:17.
37. Dewson, "Aid to the End," Dewson Papers, RL, 1:4, 5.
38. Ibid., 1:15.
39. Dewson's postelection report included a section titled, "The Opportunity Never Seized by Men," which both gave men primacy (women got opportunities men failed to seize) and also highlighted women's accomplishments (the report noted "the genius of women, and distinctly not the genius of men, is to make paper plans a reality"). Mary W. Dewson, "The Democratic National Campaign Committee, *Campaign of 1936: Work of the Women's Division*," Speeches and Articles, 1936, box 9, Dewson Papers, RL.
40. Ibid.
41. See "Publicity," in "Dewson Papers, Campaign of 1936–Publicity, General," Child Labor Amendment, Dewson Papers, RL.

42. See "Talk Given by Mary W. Dewson," Speeches and Articles, 1935, Dewson Papers, RL.

43. Ware, *Partner and I*, 204.

44. Dewson, "Aid to the End," Dewson Papers, RL, 2:179.

45. Dewson, "Letter," May 4, 1936, Buenos Aires Conference, Dewson Papers, RL.

46. Mary W. Dewson, "Important Request Made to All Our Speakers," Buenos Aires Conference, Dewson Papers, RL.

47. Dewson, "Letter," July 24, 1936, Buenos Aires Conference, Dewson Papers, RL.

48. Mary W. Dewson "Radio Parties," Buenos Aires Conference, Dewson Papers, RL.

49. Dewson, various letters, Oct. 28, 1936, Buenos Aires Conference, Dewson Papers, RL.

50. Mary W. Dewson, "A Radio Talk on Social Security," n.d., Speeches and Articles, 1936, box 9, Dewson Papers, RL.

51. Ware, *Partner and I*, 183–91. Her autobiography lists more than a hundred women who got jobs in the government. See Dewson, "Aid to the End," Dewson Papers, RL, vol. 2. She had considerable trouble with Jim Farley over patronage issues, once complaining to him that "heads you win, tails I lose." She sent a copy of that memo to Eleanor Roosevelt, from whom she received consistent support. See Mary W. Dewson, "Letter to Jim Farley," July 2, 1933, "OF 300 WD 1933–35, DNC, Dewson Folder," box 44, RL.

52. Brinkley, *Unfinished Nation*, 703; see also Downey, *Woman Behind the New Deal*, 115, and Kleinberg, "Widows' Welfare," 72.

53. Brinkley, *Unfinished Nation*, 661.

54. Emil Hurja had, for example, found evidence of a gender gap in 1932. Holli, *Wizard of Washington*, 49–51.

55. On the strikes of the 1930s, see Cashman, *America Ascendant*, 305.

56. Renshaw, "Organised Labour," 216, 222.

57. Fried, *FDR and His Enemies*, 78; Leuchtenberg, *Franklin D. Roosevelt*, 107; McElvaine, *Great Depression*, 258.

58. Downey, *Woman Behind the New Deal*, 126, 204; see also Perkins, *The Roosevelt I Knew*. Labor leaders were equally suspicious of her; see McJimsey, *Presidency*, 166.

59. On Lewis and his eventual break with FDR in 1940, see Jensen, "Thundering Voice."

60. Fried, *FDR and His Enemies*, 84.

61. Ibid., 86.

62. Brinkley, *Unfinished Nation*, 691; Renshaw, "Organised Labour," 216.

63. See Wagner, "National Labor Relations Act," Feb. 21, 1935, 71.

64. Katznelson, *Fear Itself*, 266.

65. Kennedy, *Freedom from Fear*, 301.

66. Cloud, "Null Persona."

67. Kennedy, *Freedom from Fear*, 322.

68. Katznelson, *Fear Itself*, 175.

69. Kennedy, *Freedom from Fear*, 290.

70. The White House knew about these notes almost immediately. See John Winant, "Day Letter to Mr. Arnold Berman," Oct. 23, 1936, "Social Security Act," Winant Papers, RL. Moves like this may have been one way in which "conservative businessmen and partisan Republicans may also have provided significant assistance to FDR in winning worker support." McElvaine, *Great Depression*, 116.

71. Ware, *Partner and I*, 221; "Don't Believe the Labor Spy in Your Pay Envelope," Vertical File: Campaign Literature, 1936, Democratic Labor Division, RL.

72. Kennedy, *Freedom from Fear*, 296.

73. Speech text, Oct. 23, 1936, "Miscellaneous Political Corresp, Feb–May 1936," MPC, 1935-37, box 61, Hurja Papers, RL.
74. For an example of such defense, see the correspondence between Mary W. Dewson and Arthur Altmeyer, Aug. 29, 1936, "Dem Natl Comm, Women's Div–Corresp–General–Social Security Board, 1933–1936," box 11, WD, DNC, RL.
75. *Economic Security in the Sunset of Life*, Eleanor Roosevelt Pamphlet Collection, Roosevelt, FD, Trips, Soldiers, U.S. RL.
76. See Katznelson, *Fear Itself*, 17.
77. Bunche, *Political Status*, 7.
78. Polenberg, *Era*, 29.
79. White, *FDR and the Press*, 19.
80. Such influence, for instance, kept him from supporting antilynching legislation; see Kennedy, *Freedom from Fear*, 210. Nancy J. Weiss notes that "political calculation took precedence over moral outrage" in the battle over that legislation. *Farewell*, 119.
81. Gould, *Modern American Presidency*, 91; Polenberg, *Era*, 30; Weiss, *Farewell*, 37–39.
82. Franklin D. Roosevelt, "Letter Urging the Fullest Opportunity for Exercise of the Right to Vote from the *USS Houston*," Aug. 1, 1934, in Rosenman, *Public Papers*, 3:351–52, 351. See also Roosevelt, "Radio Address from the White House," Oct. 5, 1944, in Rosenman, *Public Papers*, 13:317–25, 318.
83. His wife was immensely important in this area. See Beasley, *Eleanor Roosevelt*, 151.
84. Kennedy, *Freedom from Fear*, 208; McElvaine, *Great Depression*, 187.
85. Cashman, *America Ascendant*, 337–38.
86. For details on the Scottsboro case, see Carter, *Scottsboro*. For a discussion of communism and the fight for African American rights, see Kennedy, *Freedom from Fear*, 220–24.
87. Weiss, *Farewell*, 45.
88. Wolfskill and Hudson, *All But the People*, 87.
89. Weiss, *Farewell*, 136.
90. That the administration remained slow on racial matters did not prevent critics from charging it with proceeding too quickly. See Weiss, *Farewell*, 160–61, and Wolfskill and Hudson, *All But the People*, 169.
91. Paul W. Ward, "Wooing the Negro Vote," *Washington Weekly*, Aug. 7, 1936, 119; "Good Neighbor League, Colored Committee, Miscellaneous (1936–39)," Correspondence File, Board of Directors, Edward J. Flynn, Executive Board, John F. O'Ryan, box 1, GNL Papers, RL.
92. See Mettler, "Social Citizens," 231–71.
93. See "OF 93, Colored Matters (Negroes), 1935," box 2, RL.
94. "PPF 3412, Colored Democratic League," box PPF 3381–3421, RL.
95. *1933, the G.O.P Ship on the Rocks*, MDPC, 1–12, RL.
96. *President Hoover and Chas. G. Dawes Takes U.S. Treasury for a Ride*, MDPC, 1–12, RL.
97. "Summons to Colored Voters," Vertical File: Campaign Literature, 1936, Democratic Labor Division, RL.
98. Mary W. Dewson, "Form Letter," Sept. 15, 1936, "Folder 5: Dem Nat'l Women's Div 1935–36," General Correspondence, 1933–37, Civil Service Commission, Democratic Women's National Council, 1933–36, box 3, WD, DNC, 1933–44, RL.
99. "Memorandum for Dr. Tugwell," July 12, 1935, "Good Neighbor League, Colored Committee, Miscellaneous (1936–39)," Correspondence File, Board of Directors, Edward J. Flynn, Executive Board, John F. O'Ryan, box 1, GNL Papers, RL.
100. Adam Clayton Powell, "Letter to Edgar O. Brown," n.d., and Powell, "Telegram to Dr. Stanley High," Sept. 7, 1936, ibid.

101. Edgar O. Brown, "Memorandum to Postmaster General Farley," Feb. 26, 1936, "Miscellaneous Political Corresp, Feb–May 1936," MPC, 1935–37, box 61, Hurja Papers, RL. Hurja seems also to have been collecting similar data. See Emil Hurja, "Memo to Mrs. Duffy," July 21, 1936, "Miscellaneous Political Corresp, Feb–May 1936," Hurja Papers, MPC, 1935–37, box 61, RL.

102. Feldman, *Scorpions*; McMahon, *Reconsidering Roosevelt*; Shesol, *Supreme Power*.

103. Kleinberg, "Widows' Welfare," 72; McJimsey, *Presidency*, 108.

104. Mettler, "Social Citizens," 233, 253. See also Davis, "Unsuspected Radicalism," 56.

105. Mileur, "Boss," 121.

106. There are arguments to be made that Roosevelt, especially through his appointments to the United States Supreme Court, did considerably more to advance the interests of African Americans in the long term. See especially, McMahon, *Reconsidering Roosevelt*. See also McElvaine, *Great Depression*, 188.

107. McJimsey, *Presidency*, 142.

108. Shlaes, *Forgotten Man*, 11.

109. This is one of Sidney M. Milkis's most consistent arguments; see, for example, *President and the Parties*. For an application of this idea to interest-group politics in particular, see Leuchtenberg, *Franklin D. Roosevelt*, 87. For the best analysis of the ways in which independence from the party led to dependence on bureaucracy, see Milkis, "Franklin D. Roosevelt."

Chapter 4

1. Tulis, *Rhetorical Presidency*. But see also Lim, "Presidency and the Media."

2. Drury, *People's Voice*, 2.

3. Farrell, *Norms of Rhetorical Culture*, 85, 86.

4. Stuckey, *Good Neighbor*.

5. Maney, *Roosevelt Presence*, 84–86. See also McElvaine, *Great Depression*, 254.

6. On the unifying and divisive potential of the 1936 campaign, see Leuchtenberg, *Franklin D. Roosevelt*, 170.

7. In my view, this depiction had a great deal to do with the idea that Roosevelt's rhetoric was "intimate." Elvin T. Lim finds no language in the Fireside Chats that would explain this feeling of intimacy. See "Lion and the Lamb."

8. Scott Welsh, for instance, argues that the fictions of security and citizen empowerment are inimical to understanding how democracy actually works. See *Rhetorical Surface*.

9. For a contemporaneous discussion of the communicative tendencies of the 1936 election, see Oliver, "Electionisms of 1936."

10. See, for example, a memo outlining the various aspects of a media campaign and assigning duties for speech material and media relations, the content of pamphlets, radio policy, and plans for organizing businessmen. The memo concludes, "I should like to glance personally at this publicity before it is decided on." Franklin D. Roosevelt, "Memo to Jim Farley," Mar. 26, 1936, "OF 300, Stanley High," box 45, DNC, RL.

11. On the machinations behind changing the two-thirds rule and for a brief discussion of its significance, see Farley, *Behind the Ballots*, 307.

12. Aide Jim Farley called Roosevelt's speech "the greatest piece of personal campaigning in American history." Ibid., 316.

13. Gosnell, *Champion Campaigner*, 140.

14. Franklin D. Roosevelt, "Annual Message to Congress," Jan. 3, 1936, in Rosenman, *Public Papers*, 5:8–18, 9, 12.

15. Ibid., 5:12.
16. Ibid., 5:13.
17. Ibid., 5:13, 14.
18. Franklin D. Roosevelt, "Address at Little Rock, Arkansas," June 10, 1936, in Rosenman, *Public Papers*, 5:195–202, 199; Franklin D. Roosevelt, "Acceptance of the Renomination for the Presidency," June 27, 1936, in Rosenman, *Public Papers*, 5:230–36, 233.
19. Franklin D. Roosevelt, "Address at the Jackson Day Dinner," Jan. 8, 1936, in Rosenman, *Public Papers*, 5:38–44, 39.
20. Franklin D. Roosevelt, "Address at the Thomas Jefferson Dinner, New York City," Apr. 25, 1936, in Rosenman, *Public Papers*, 5:177–82, 178.
21. Franklin D. Roosevelt, "Radio Address on Brotherhood Day," Feb. 23, 1936, in Rosenman, *Public Papers*, 5:85–87, 85.
22. For a more detailed discussion of the effects of the Judeo-Christian tradition, as it extended across Roosevelt's entire presidency, see Stuckey, *Good Neighbor*, chap. 1, quote on page 86.
23. Franklin D. Roosevelt, "Address to the Young Democrats, Baltimore, Maryland," Apr. 13, 1936, in Rosenman, *Public Papers*, 5:159–66, 159, 161, 165.
24. Leuchtenberg notes that "Roosevelt campaigned in 1936 as the leader of a liberal crusade which knew no party lines." *Franklin D. Roosevelt*, 190.
25. Roosevelt, "Jackson Day Dinner," 39.
26. Franklin D. Roosevelt, "Address at Temple University," Feb. 22, 1936, Philadelphia, in Rosenman, *Public Papers*, 5:80–84, 84.
27. Stanley High, "A Republican Takes a Walk," *Forum*, May 1936, 5–7, "OF 300, Stanley High," box 45, DNC, RL, 5, 6.
28. *Life* picked up on the class theme: its October 1936 cover featured a woman in the back seat of a chauffeur-driven car wearing a Landon button; in the front seat sit two chauffeurs, both wearing FDR buttons. "Scrapbook," Dewson Papers, RL.
29. Franklin D. Roosevelt, "A Greeting to Labor's Non-Partisan League," Aug. 3, 1936, in Rosenman, *Public Papers*, 5:280–81, 280.
30. Burke, *Grammar of Motives*, 3–15.
31. Greer, *What Roosevelt Thought*, 19.
32. Franklin D. Roosevelt, "Address at Dallas, Texas," June 12, 1936, in Rosenman, *Public Papers*, 5:209–14, 211–12.
33. Roosevelt, "Thomas Jefferson Dinner," 181.
34. Greer, *What Roosevelt Thought*, 38–39.
35. Dewson, "Radio Talk," Dewson Papers, RL.
36. "Security and Liberty," Scripps Howard, n.d., "Speech Material: National Politics" and "Speech Material: National Debt," PPF 1820, RL.
37. Greer, *What Roosevelt Thought*, 45.
38. Jenkins, *Franklin Delano Roosevelt*, 90.
39. Franklin D. Roosevelt, introd. to Rosenman, *Public Papers*, 5:3–7, 3.
40. Roosevelt, "Annual Message," 14.
41. Roosevelt, "Acceptance of the Renomination," 232.
42. Franklin D. Roosevelt, "Address Delivered at Democratic State Convention, Syracuse, New York," Sept. 29, 1936, in Rosenman, *Public Papers*, 5:383–92, 385.
43. Fried, *FDR and His Enemies*, 123.
44. There is some proof that the anecdotal evidence provided better information than the polls; Jim Farley, who relied on a vast web of personal connections, predicted the election results with more accuracy than Hurja.

45. Webber, *New Deal Fat Cats*, 7–9.
46. Fried, *FDR and His Enemies*, 6; Perkins, *The Roosevelt I Knew*, 155.
47. Webber, *New Deal Fat Cats*, 21.
48. Edgar Eugene Robinson made a similar point in 1947. See Robinson, *They Voted for Roosevelt*, v.
49. Gosnell, *Champion Campaigner*, 156.
50. Stephenson, *Campaigns and the Court*, 138.
51. Commentators had predicted that the Court would be a major issue in 1936; they were wrong. Ibid., 149.
52. Shesol, *Supreme Power*, 107–9.
53. Herbert Hoover and Al Smith rank high on this list. On Hoover, see the letter from Louis Howe to Mr. Niven, Sept. 14, 1934, and attached articles, OF 1150, ALL, Sept. 1934, RL. On Smith and the league, see Fried, *FDR and His Enemies*, 120–25.
54. Schlesinger, *Age of Roosevelt*, 567.
55. Letter from Isodore Shaffer to Jouett Shouse, copied and sent to FDR with "Aside to the President: Appended." OF 1150, ALL, 1936–37, RL. Emphasis in original.
56. According to Jim Farley, FDR considered these surrogates part of an "aggressive" campaign strategy. Farley, *Jim Farley's Story*, 57.
57. Dewson, "Aid to the End," Dewson Papers, RL, 2:97–127.
58. Leuchtenberg, *Franklin D. Roosevelt*, 177.
59. Alf Landon, "Acceptance Speech," July 23, 1936, *Kansapedia*, Kansas Historical Society, www.kshs.org/kansapedia/alfred-landon-s-acceptance-speech/14501, 1, 2.
60. Ibid., 2.
61. Ibid.
62. Ibid.
63. This argument was in keeping with a long history of political economic thought and had been largely accepted by both parties prior to the Depression. See Stuckey, *Defining Americans*, 106–50.
64. Gosnell, *Champion Campaigner*, 164.
65. McElvaine, *Great Depression*, 257.
66. Smith, *FDR*, 365.
67. Leuchtenberg, *Franklin D. Roosevelt*, 181–83.
68. See the campaign material found in "Dewson Collection, Campaign Literature–Republicans" and "Dewson Collection, Campaign Literature–Democrats," MDPC, 1–12, RL.
69. See, for example, "The Farmer Remembers Longer Than the Elephant," in "Scrapbook," Dewson Papers, RL.
70. Reorganization Committee of the Republican Party of Cook County, Illinois, "Declaration of Principles," in "Speech Material: National Politics" and "Speech Material: National Debt," PPF 1820, RL.
71. George Wharton Pepper, "What Are We Going to Do About It?" "Speech Material: National Politics" and "Speech Material: National Debt," PPF 1820, RL, 1.
72. Ibid., 3, 5.
73. Arthur Krock, for example, noted the enthusiasm with which Republicans greeted words like "holy" and "crusade" at their convention. See "A Further Analysis Is Made of the Republican Platform," June 18, 1936, "Speech Material: Platform" and "Speech Material: National Debt," PPF 1820, RL.
74. Pepper, "Going to Do," 6, 8.
75. See Walter Lippmann, "The 1936 Platform: II Republicans," *New York Post*, June 16, 1936, in "Speech Material: Platform" and "Speech Material: National Debt," PPF 1820, RL.

76. Brinkley, *Unfinished Nation*, 696; Webber, *New Deal Fat Cats*, 127.
77. McElvaine, *Great Depression*, 282; Webber, *New Deal Fat Cats*, 133.
78. Gosnell, *Champion Campaigner*, 166.
79. Leuchtenberg, *Franklin D. Roosevelt*, 190.

Conclusion

1. Leuchtenberg, *Franklin D. Roosevelt*, 347.
2. Jonathan Alter argues that "Obama saw [the election] less as a struggle between conservatives and liberals than a fight between right-wing extremism and pragmatic centrism." See the chapters "Shellacking" and "New Chicago Machine," both in Alter's *Center Holds*. Roosevelt could have said much the same thing in 1936.
3. One way to understand this is by looking at their mandate rhetoric. See Azari, *Delivering the People's Message*.
4. On FDR and the Court, see Feldman, *Scorpions*; McMahon, *Reconsidering Roosevelt*; and Shesol, *Supreme Power*. On the party system, see Milkis and Mileur, *New Deal*.
5. Kennedy, *Freedom from Fear*, 285; Polenberg, introd. to *Era*, 14.
6. Clyde P. Weed, for instance, argues that the images from that election continue to color our understanding of the political parties today. See *Transformation*. On the centrality of the 1936 election to the New Deal, see Burnham, *Critical Elections*. On the importance of the New Deal to American politics, see Katznelson, *Fear Itself*; Stephenson, *Campaigns and the Court*, 154; and Webber, *New Deal Fat Cats*, 10.
7. But see Leuchtenberg, *Franklin D. Roosevelt*, 327.
8. Roosevelt signed Executive Order 8248, establishing the Executive Office of the President, in September 1939. For details, see the information available through the Federal Register: "Executive Order 8248: Establishing the Divisions of the Executive Office of the President and Defining Their Functions and Duties," Sept. 8, 1939, National Archives, fhttp://www.archives.gov/federal-register/codification/executive-order/08248.html.
9. The modern presidency conventionally begins with Roosevelt. See, among many others, Greenstein, *Modern Presidency*.
10. Leuchtenberg, *Franklin D. Roosevelt*, 331–32.
11. Shlaes, *Forgotten Man*, 10–11.
12. Leuchtenberg, *Shadow of FDR*.
13. Alter, "Shellacking," in *Center Holds*.
14. Edwards, *On Deaf Ears*; Edwards, *Strategic Presidency*. But see also arguments with and modifications of his conclusions in J. Cohen, *Going Local*, and Wood, *Presidential Representation*.
15. On the relationship of the New Deal to the Progressives, see Hofstadter, *Age of Reform*, 307–17.
16. Dewson, "Aid to the End," Dewson Papers, RL, vol. 2.
17. "The 2012 Money Race: Compare the Candidates," *New York Times*, 2012, http://elections.nytimes.com/2012/campaign-finance.
18. This was, however, changing even in the 1930s. The media did cover the private lives of his children, including their marital woes, and he and Eleanor generated far more coverage of their lives than had the Hoovers.
19. "Mitt Romney's '47%' Comments: A History-Video," October 5, 2012, *Guardian*, www.theguardian.com/world/video/2012/oct/05/romney-47-percent-remarks-history-video.
20. Farrell, *Norms of Rhetorical Culture*, 85.

BIBLIOGRAPHY

Alter, Jonathan. *The Center Holds: Obama and His Enemies*. New York: Simon and Schuster, 2013.
———. *The Defining Moment: FDR's Hundred Days and the Triumph of Hope*. New York: Simon and Schuster.
Althaus, Scott L. *Collective Preference in Democratic Politics: Opinion Surveys and the Will of the People*. New York: Cambridge University Press, 2003.
Arnold, Peri. *Making the Managerial Presidency: Comprehensive Reorganization Planning, 1905–1996*. Lawrence: University Press of Kansas, 1998.
Asen, Robert. "A Discourse Theory of Citizenship." *Quarterly Journal of Speech* 90 (2004): 189–211.
———. "Toward a Normative Conception of Difference in Public Deliberation." *Argumentation and Advocacy* 35 (1999): 115–29.
Atwill, Janet M. "Rhetoric and Civic Virtue." In *The Viability of the Rhetorical Tradition*, edited by Richard Graff, Arthur E. Walzer, and Janet M. Atwill, 75–94. Albany: SUNY Press, 2005.
Azari, Julia R. *Delivering the People's Message: The Changing Politics of the Presidential Mandate*. Ithaca: Cornell University Press, 2014.
Badger, Anthony J. *FDR: The First Hundred Days*. New York: Hill and Wang, 2008.
———. "Huey Long and the New Deal." In Baskerville and Willett, *Nothing Else to Fear*, 64–103.
Baskerville, Stephen W., and Ralph Willett, eds. *Nothing Else to Fear: New Perspectives on America in the Thirties*. Dover, N.H.: Manchester University Press, 1985.
Beasley, Maurine H. *Eleanor Roosevelt: Transformative First Lady*. Lawrence: University Press of Kansas, 2010.
Beasley, Vanessa, and Deborah Smith-Howell. "No Ordinary Rhetorical President: FDR's Speechmaking and Leadership." In Benson, *American Rhetoric*, 1–32.
Benson, Thomas W., ed. *American Rhetoric in the New Deal Era, 1932–1945*. East Lansing: Michigan State University Press, 2006.
Berinsky, Adam J., ed. *New Directions in Public Opinion*. New York: Routledge, 2012.
Best, Gary Dean. *The Critical Press and the New Deal: The Press Versus Presidential Power, 1933–1938*. Westport, Conn.: Praeger, 1993.
Black, Conrad. *Franklin Delano Roosevelt: Champion of Freedom*. New York: Public Affairs, 2003.
Brands, H. W. *Traitor to His Class: The Privileged Life and Radical Presidency of Franklin Delano Roosevelt*. New York: Doubleday, 2008.
Brinkley, Alan. *Franklin Delano Roosevelt*. New York: Oxford, 2010.
———. *The Unfinished Nation: A Concise History of the American People*. New York: McGraw-Hill, 1993.

Bunche, Ralph Johnson. *The Political Status of the Negro in the Age of FDR*. Chicago: University of Chicago Press, 1973.
Burke, Kenneth. *A Grammar of Motives*. Berkeley: University of California Press, 1969.
Burner, David. *Herbert Hoover: A Public Life*. New York: Knopf, 1979.
Burnham, Walter Dean. *Critical Elections and the Mainsprings of American Politics*. New York: Norton, 1970.
Burns, James MacGregor. *Roosevelt: The Lion and the Fox, 1882–1940*. New York: Harcourt Brace Jovanovich, 1956.
Carlisle, Rodney P. *Hearst and the New Deal: The Progressive as Reactionary*. New York: Garland, 1979.
Carpenter, Ronald H. "Father Charles E. Coughlin: Delivery, Style in Discourse, and Opinion Leadership." In Benson, *American Rhetoric*, 315–67.
Carter, Dan T. *Scottsboro: A Tragedy of the American South*. Baton Rouge: Louisiana State University Press, 2007.
Cashman, Sean Dennis. *America Ascendant: From Theodore Roosevelt to FDR in the Century of American Power, 1901–1945*. New York: NYU Press, 1998.
Ceaser, James W., Glen E. Thurow, Jeffrey Tulis, and Joseph E. Bessette. "The Rise of the Rhetorical Presidency." *Presidential Studies Quarterly* 11 (1981): 158–71.
Cloud, Dana. "The Null Persona: Race and the Rhetoric of Violence in the Uprising of '34." *Rhetoric and Public Affairs* 2 (1999): 177–209.
Cohen, Adam. *Nothing to Fear: FDR's Inner Circle and the Hundred Days That Created Modern America*. New York: Penguin, 2009.
Cohen, Jeffrey E. *Going Local: Presidential Leadership in the Post-Broadcast Age*. New York: Cambridge University Press, 2010.
Dalleck, Robert. *Hail to the Chief: The Making and Unmaking of American Presidents*. New York: Hyperion, 1996.
Davis, Gareth. "The Unsuspected Radicalism of the Social Security Act." In Garson and Kidd, *Roosevelt Years*, 56–57.
Delli Carpini, Michael X., Fay Lomax Cook, and Lawrence Jacobs. "Public Deliberation, Discursive Participation, and Citizen Engagement: A Review of the Literature." *Annual Review of Political Science* 7 (2004): 315–44.
Downey, Kirstin. *The Woman Behind the New Deal: The Life and Legacy of Frances Perkins; Social Security, Unemployment Insurance, and the Minimum Wage*. New York: Anchor, 2010.
Drury, Jeffrey P. Mehltretter. *Speaking with the People's Voice: How Presidents Invoke Public Opinion*. College Station: Texas A&M University Press, 2014.
Edsforth, Ronald. *The New Deal: America's Response to the Great Depression*. Malden, Mass.: Blackwell, 2000.
Edwards, George C., III. *On Deaf Ears: The Limits of the Bully Pulpit*. New Haven, Conn.: Yale University Press, 2006.
———. *The Strategic President: Persuasion and Opportunity in Presidential Leadership*. Princeton: Princeton University Press, 2009.
Eisenach, Eldon J. *Sacred Discourse and American Nationality*. Lanham, Md.: Rowman and Littlefield, 2012.
Eisinger, Robert M. *The Evolution of Presidential Polling*. New York: Cambridge University Press, 2003.
Eliot, Thomas H. *Recollections of the New Deal: When People Mattered*. Boston: Northeastern University Press, 1992.

Farley, James A. *Behind the Ballots: The Personal History of a Politician.* New York: Harcourt, Brace, 1938.
———. *Jim Farley's Story: The Roosevelt Years.* New York: Whittlesey House, 1948.
Farrell, Thomas B. *Norms of Rhetorical Culture.* New Haven: Yale University Press, 1993.
Fausold, Martin L. *The Presidency of Herbert C. Hoover.* Lawrence: University Press of Kansas, 1985.
Feinman, Ronald L. *Twilight of Progressivism: The Western Republican Senators and the New Deal.* Baltimore: Johns Hopkins University Press, 1981.
Feldman, Noah. *Scorpions: The Battles and Triumphs of FDR's Great Supreme Court Justices.* New York, Twelve, 2010.
Flynn, George Q. *American Catholics and the Roosevelt Presidency, 1932–1936.* Lexington: University of Kentucky Press, 1968.
Flynn, John T. *As We Go Marching.* New York: Arno, 1972.
———. *Country Squire in the White House.* New York: Doubleday, 1940.
———. *The Roosevelt Myth.* New York: Devin-Adair, 1948.
Folsom, Burton W. *New Deal or Raw Deal? How FDR's Economic Legacy Has Damaged America.* New York: Threshold, 2008.
Fried, Albert. *FDR and His Enemies.* New York: St. Martin's Press, 1999.
Friedel, Frank. *F. D. R. and the South.* Baton Rouge: Louisiana State University Press, 1965.
Fusfeld, Daniel R. *The Economic Thought of Franklin D. Roosevelt: The Origins of the New Deal.* New York: Columbia University Press, 1956.
Gallup, George H. *The Gallup Poll: Public Opinion, 1935–1971.* New York: Random House, 1972.
Garson, Robert A., and Stuart S. Kidd, eds. *The Roosevelt Years: New Perspectives on American History, 1933–1945.* Edinburgh: Edinburgh University Press, 1999.
Gastil, John. *By Popular Demand: Revitalizing Representative Democracy Through Deliberative Elections.* Berkeley: University of California Press, 2000.
Green, Jeffrey Edward. *The Eyes of the People: Democracy in an Age of Spectatorship.* New York: Oxford University Press, 2007.
Greenstein, Fred, I., ed. *Leadership in the Modern Presidency.* Cambridge, Mass.: Harvard University Press, 1988.
Golway, Terry, *Together We Cannot Fail: FDR and the American Presidency in Years of Crisis.* Naperville, Ill.: Sourcebooks, 2009.
Gosnell, Harold F. *Champion Campaigner: Franklin D. Roosevelt.* New York: Macmillan, 1952.
Gould, Lewis L. *The Modern American Presidency.* Lawrence: University Press of Kansas, 2003.
Greer, Thomas H. *What Roosevelt Thought: The Social and Political Ideas of Franklin D. Roosevelt.* East Lansing: Michigan State University Press, 1958.
Gunther, John. *Roosevelt in Retrospect.* New York: Harper and Brothers, 1950.
Hamby, Alonzo L. *For the Survival of Democracy: Franklin Roosevelt and the World Crisis of the 1930s.* New York: Free Press, 2004.
Hanson, Russell L. *The Democratic Imagination in America: Conversations with Our Past.* Princeton: Princeton University Press, 1985.
Hauser, Gerard A. "Vernacular Dialogue and the Rhetoricality of Public Opinion." *Communications Monographs* 65 (1998): 83–107.
———. *Vernacular Voices: The Rhetoric of Publics and Public Spheres.* Columbia: University of South Carolina Press, 1999.
Hauser, Gerard A., and Gerald C. Benoit-Barne. "Reflections on Rhetoric: Deliberative Democracy, Civil Society, and Trust." *Rhetoric and Public Affairs* 5 (2002): 261–75.

Herbst, Susan. *Numbered Voices: How Opinion Polling Has Shaped American Politics*. Chicago: University of Chicago Press, 1993.

Herzstein, Robert Edwin, *Roosevelt and Hitler: Prelude to War*. New York: Paragon House, 1989.

Hofstadter, Richard. *The Age of Reform*. New York: Vintage, 1955.

Hogan, J. Michael. "George Gallup and the Rhetoric of Scientific Democracy." *Communication Monographs* 64 (1987): 161–79.

———. "The 'Science' of Cold War Strategy: Propaganda and Public Opinion in the Eisenhower Administration's 'War of Words.'" In Medhurst and Brands, *Critical Reflections*, 134–68.

Hogan, J. Michael, George C. Edwards III, Wynton C. Hall, Christine L. Harold, Gerard A. Hauser, Susan Herbst, Robert Y. Shapiro, and Ted J. Smith. "Report of the National Task Force on the Presidency and Public Opinion." In *The Prospect of Presidential Rhetoric*, edited by Martin J. Medhurst and James Arnt Aune, 293–316. College Station: Texas A&M University Press.

Hogan, J. Michael, and Glen Williams. "The Rusticity and Religiosity of Huey P. Long." *Rhetoric and Public Affairs* 7 (2004): 149–72.

Holli, Melvin G. *The Wizard of Washington: Emil Hurja, Franklin Roosevelt, and the Birth of Public Opinion Polling*. New York: Palgrave, 2002.

Hopkins, Harry. "Federal Relief." In Polenberg, *Era*, 83–89.

Howard, Thomas C., and William D. Pederson, eds. *Franklin D. Roosevelt and the Formation of the Modern World*. Armonk, N.Y.: Sharpe, 2003.

Huizinga, Johan. *Homo Ludens: A Short Study of the Play Element in Culture*. New York: Routledge, 2008.

Hurd, Charles. *When the New Deal Was Young and Gay*. New York: Hawthorn Books, 1965.

Ickes, Harold L. *The Secret Diary of Harold L. Ickes*. Vol. 2, *The Inside Struggle, 1936–1939*. New York: Simon and Schuster, 1954.

Iltis, Robert S. "Reconsidering the Demagoguery of Huey Long." In Benson, *American Rhetoric*, 369–417.

Jackson, Robert H. *That Man: An Insider's Portrait of Franklin D. Roosevelt*. New York: Oxford University Press, 2003.

Janeway, Michael. *The Fall of the House of Roosevelt: Brokers of Ideas and Power from FDR to LBJ*. New York: Columbia University Press, 2004.

Jenkins, Roy. *Franklin Delano Roosevelt*. New York: Holt, 2003.

Jenner, Robert E. *FDR's Republicans: Domestic Political Realignment and American Foreign Policy*. Lanham, Md.: Lexington Books, 2010.

Jensen, Richard J. "The Thundering Voice of John L. Lewis." In Benson, *American Rhetoric*, 279–314.

Josephson, Matthew. *Infidel in the Temple: A Memoir of the Nineteen-Thirties*. New York: Knopf, 1967.

Kanawada, Leo V., Jr. *Franklin D. Roosevelt's Diplomacy and American Catholics, Italians, and Jews*. Ann Arbor: UMI Research Press, 1980.

Katznelson, Ira. *Fear Itself: The New Deal and the Origins of Our Time*. New York: Liveright, 2013.

Keller, Morton. "The New Deal and Progressivism." In Milkis and Mileur, *Triumph of Liberalism*, 313–22.

Kennedy, David M. *Freedom from Fear: The American People in Depression and War, 1929–1945*. New York: Oxford University Press, 1999.

Kessler-Harris, Alice. *In Pursuit of Equity: Women, Men, and the Quest for Economic Citizenship in Twentieth-Century America*. New York: Oxford University Press, 2001.
———. *Out to Work: A History of Wage-Earning Women in the United States*. New York: Oxford University Press, 2003.
King, Desmond S., and Rogers M. Smith. *Still a House Divided: Race and Politics in Obama's America*. Princeton: Princeton University Press, 2011.
Kleinberg, S. Jay. "Widows' Welfare in the Great Depression." In Garson and Kidd, *Roosevelt Years*, 72–90.
Kock, Christian, and Lisa Villasden, eds. *Rhetorical Citizenship and Public Deliberation*. University Park: Pennsylvania State University Press, 2012.
Landon, Alfred A. "I Will Not Promise the Moon." October 15, 1936. *History Matters: The U.S. Survey Course on the Web*. http://historymatters.gmu.edu/d/8128/.
Landy, Marc. "Presidential Party Leadership and Party Realignment: FDR and the Making of the New Deal Democratic Party." In Milkis and Mileur, *Triumph of Liberalism*, 73–85.
Lash, Joseph P. *Dealers and Dreamers: A New Look at the New Deal*. New York: Doubleday, 1988.
Leuchtenberg, William Edward. *Franklin D. Roosevelt and the New Deal*. New York: Harper Perennial, 1961.
———. *In the Shadow of FDR: From Harry Truman to Bill Clinton*. 2nd ed. Ithaca: Cornell University Press, 1993.
Lim, Elvin T. *The Anti-Intellectual Presidency: The Decline of Presidential Rhetoric from George Washington to George W. Bush*. Oxford: Oxford University Press, 2008.
———. "Five Trends in Presidential Rhetoric: An Analysis of Rhetoric from George Washington to Bill Clinton." *Presidential Studies Quarterly* 32 (2002): 228–45.
———. "The Lion and the Lamb: De-mythologizing Franklin Roosevelt's Fireside Chats." *Rhetoric and Public Affairs* 6, no. 3 (2003): 437–64.
———. "The Presidency and the Media: Two Faces of Democracy." In *The Presidency and the Political System*, edited by Michael Nelson, 258–71. 10th ed. Washington, D.C.: CQ Press, 2013.
Lindley, Ernest K. *The Roosevelt Revolution: First Phase*. New York: Viking, 1933.
Lippmann, Walter. "Agriculture and the National Interest." In Lippmann, *Interpretations*, 82–86.
———. "The G.O.P., April 4, 1935." In Lippmann, *Interpretations*, 275–77.
———. "Huey Long's Power." In Lippmann, *Interpretations*, 272–74.
———. *Interpretations: 1933–1935*. Edited by Allan Nevins. New York: Macmillan, 1936.
———. "On Making Things Too Complicated." In Lippmann, *Interpretations*, 256–59.
Lowi, Theodore J. *The End of Liberalism: The Second Republic of the United States*. 40th anniversary ed. New York: Norton, 2009.
———. *The Personal President: Power Invested, Promise Unfulfilled*. Ithaca: Cornell University Press, 1986.
Maney, Patrick J. *The Roosevelt Presence: A Biography of Franklin Delano Roosevelt*. New York: Twayne, 1992.
McCoy, Donald R. *Angry Voices: Left-of-Center Politics in the New Deal Era*. Port Washington, N.Y.: Kennikat Press, 1958.
McElvaine, Robert S. *The Great Depression: America, 1929–1941*. New York: Three Rivers Press, 2009.
McJimsey, George. *The Presidency of Franklin Delano Roosevelt*. Lawrence: University Press of Kansas, 2000.

McMahon, Kevin J. *Reconsidering Roosevelt on Race: How the Presidency Paved the Road to Brown*. Chicago: University of Chicago Press, 2004.

Medhurst, Martin J. "Argument and Role: Monsignor John A. Ryan on Social Justice." *Western Journal of Speech Communication* 52 (Winter 1988): 75–90.

———, ed. *A Rhetorical History of the United States*. Vol. 8, *World War II and the Cold War*. East Lansing: Michigan State University Press, forthcoming.

Medhurst, Martin J., and H. W. Brands, eds. *Critical Reflections on the Cold War: Linking Rhetoric and History*. College Station: Texas A&M University Press, 2000.

Mettler, Suzette. "Social Citizens of Separate Sovereignties: Governance in the New Deal Welfare State." In Milkis and Mileur, *Triumph of Liberalism*, 231–71.

Mileur, Jerome M. "'The Boss': Franklin Roosevelt, the Democratic Party, and the Reconstitution of American Politics." In Milkis and Mileur, *Triumph of Liberalism*, 86–134.

Milkis, Sidney M. "Franklin D. Roosevelt, the Economic Constitutional Order, and the New Politics of Presidential Leadership." In Milkis and Mileur, *Triumph of Liberalism*, 31–72.

———. "Introduction: Progressivism Then and Now." In Milkis and Mileur, *Progressivism*, 1–39.

———. *Political Parties and Constitutional Government: Remaking American Democracy*. Baltimore: Johns Hopkins University Press, 1999.

———. *The President and the Parties: The Transformation of the American Party System Since the New Deal*. New York: Oxford University Press, 1993.

———. *Theodore Roosevelt, the Progressive Party, and the Transformation of American Democracy*. Lawrence: University Press of Kansas, 2009.

Milkis, Sidney M., and Jerome M. Mileur, eds. *The New Deal and the Triumph of Liberalism*. Amherst: University of Massachusetts Press, 2002.

———. *Progressivism and the New Democracy*. Amherst: University of Massachusetts Press, 1999.

Moley, Raymond. Introduction to Baskerville and Willett, *Nothing Else to Fear*, 1–12.

Oliver, Robert T. "Electionisms of 1936." *American Speech* 12 (1937): 3–9.

Olson, Lynne. *Those Angry Days: Roosevelt, Lindbergh, and America's Fight over World War II, 1939–1941*. New York: Random House, 2014.

Parker, Stamford. *Words That Reshaped America: FDR*. New York: Harper, 2000.

Perkins, Frances. *The Roosevelt I Knew*. New York: Viking, 1946.

Philp, Kenneth R., ed. *Indian Self-Rule: First-Hand Accounts of Indian-White Relations from Roosevelt to Reagan*. Logan: Utah State University Press, 1995.

Polenberg, Richard. *The Era of Franklin D. Roosevelt, 1933–1945: A Brief History with Documents*. New York: Bedford/St. Martin's Press, 2000.

Powell, Jim. *FDR's Folly: How Roosevelt and His New Deal Prolonged the Great Depression*. New York: Crown Forum, 2003.

Renshaw, Patrick. "Organised Labour and the Keynesian Revolution." In Baskerville and Willett, *Nothing Else to Fear*, 216–35.

Ribuffo, Leo P. *The Old Christian Right: The Protestant Far Right from the Great Depression to the Cold War*. Philadelphia: Temple University Press, 1983.

Robinson, Edgar Eugene. *They Voted for Roosevelt: The Presidential Vote, 1932–1944*. Stanford: Stanford University Press, 1947.

Rosenman, Samuel I., ed. *The Public Papers and Addresses of Franklin D. Roosevelt*. 6 vols. New York: Random House, 1938.

———. *Working with Roosevelt*. New York: Harper and Brothers, 1952.

Roth, Benjamin. *The Great Depression: A Diary*. Edited by James Ledbetter and Daniel B. Roth. New York: Public Affairs, 2009.

Ryan, Halford R. *Franklin D. Roosevelt's Rhetorical Presidency*. New York: Greenwood, 1988.
Scharf, Lois, and Joan M. Jensen. *Decades of Discontent: The Women's Movement, 1920–1940*. Westport, Conn.: Greenwood, 1983.
Schlesinger, Arthur M., Jr. *The Age of Roosevelt: The Coming of the New Deal, 1933–1935*. New York: Houghton Mifflin, 1959.
Scroop, Daniel. *Mr. Democrat: Jim Farley, the New Deal, and the Making of Modern American Politics*. Ann Arbor: University of Michigan Press, 2006.
Shafer, Byron E., ed. *The End of Realignment? Interpreting American Electoral Eras*. Madison: University of Wisconsin Press, 1991.
Shesol, Jeff. *Supreme Power: Franklin Roosevelt vs. the Supreme Court*. New York: Norton, 2010.
Shlaes, Amity. *The Forgotten Man: A New History of the Great Depression*. New York: Harper, 2007.
Shogan, Robert. *Prelude to Catastrophe: FDR's Jews and the Menace of Nazism*. New York: Ivan R. Dee, 2010.
Skocpol, Theda. *Diminished Democracy: From Membership to Management in American Civic Life*. Norman: University of Oklahoma Press, 2003.
Skowronek, Stephen. *The Politics Presidents Make: Leadership from John Adams to Bill Clinton*. Rev. ed. Cambridge, Mass.: Belknap Press of Harvard University Press, 1997.
Sloan, John W. *FDR and Reagan: Transformative Presidents with Clashing Visions*. Lawrence: University Press of Kansas, 2008.
Smith, Jean Edward. *FDR*. New York: Random House, 2007.
Smith, Ted J., and Michael J. Hogan. "Public Opinion and the Panama Canal Treaties of 1977." *Public Opinion Quarterly* 51 (1987): 5–30.
Stephenson, Douglas Greer. *Campaigns and the Court: The U.S. Supreme Court in Presidential Elections*. New York: Columbia University Press, 1999.
Stuckey, Mary E. *Defining Americans: The Presidency and National Identity*. Lawrence: University Press of Kansas, 2004.
———. *The Good Neighbor: Franklin D. Roosevelt and the Rhetoric of American Power*. East Lansing: Michigan State University Press, 2013.
———. "The 'Great Debate': The Battle over American Neutrality, 1936–1941." In Medhurst, *Rhetorical History*.
Takaki, Ronald. *A Different Mirror: A History of Multicultural America*. Boston: Back Bay Books, 1993.
Taylor, Graham D. *The New Deal and American Indian Tribalism: The Administration of the Indian Reorganization Act, 1934–45*. Lincoln: University of Nebraska Press, 1980.
"Townsend Plan Movement." *Social Security History*. Accessed November 4, 2014. www.ssa.gov/history/towns5.html.
Tugwell, Rexford G. *In Search of Roosevelt*. Cambridge, Mass.: Harvard University Press, 1972.
Tulis, Jeffrey. *The Rhetorical Presidency*. Princeton: Princeton University Press, 1987.
Unofficial Observer [John Franklin Carter]. *American Messiahs*. New York: Simon and Schuster, 1935.
Venn, Fiona. *The New Deal*. Edinburgh: Edinburgh University Press, 1998.
Wagner, Robert E. "The National Labor Relations Act." In Polenberg, *Era*, 68–72.
Waisanen, Don. "Toward Robust Public Engagement: The Value of *Deliberative* Discourse for *Civil* Communication." *Rhetoric and Public Affairs* 17 (2014): 287–322.
Walcott, Charles E., and Karen M. Hult. *Governing the White House: From Hoover Through LBJ*. Lawrence: University Press of Kansas. 1995.

Wandersee, Winifred D. *Women's Work and Family Values, 1920–1940*. Cambridge, Mass.: Harvard University Press, 1981.
Ware, Susan. *Beyond Suffrage: Women in the New Deal*. Cambridge, Mass.: Harvard University Press, 1981.
———. *Partner and I: Molly Dewson, Feminism, and New Deal Politics*. New Haven: Yale University Press, 1987.
Webber, Michael J. *New Deal Fat Cats: Business, Labor, and Campaign Finance in the 1936 Presidential Election*. New York: Fordham University Press, 2000.
Weed, Clyde P. *The Transformation of the Republican Party, 1912–1936: From Reform to Resistance*. Boulder: First Forum Press, 2012.
Weiss, Nancy J. *Farewell to the Party of Lincoln: Black Politics in the Age of FDR*. Princeton: Princeton University Press, 1983.
Welsh, Scott. *The Rhetorical Surface of Democracy: How Deliberative Ideals Undermine Democratic Politics*. Lanham, Md.: Lexington Books, 2013.
White, Graham J. *FDR and the Press*. Chicago: University of Chicago Press, 1979.
Wilson, Joan Hoff. *Herbert Hoover: Forgotten Progressive*. Boston: Little, Brown, 1975.
Wolfskill, George, and John A. Hudson, eds. *All But the People: Franklin D. Roosevelt and His Critics, 1933–1939*. New York: Macmillan, 1969.
Wood, B. Dan. *The Myth of Presidential Representation*. New York: Cambridge University Press, 2009.
Yarsinske, Amy Waters. *Rendezvous with Destiny: The FDR Legacy*. Virginia Beach: Dunning, 2009.
Young, Iris Marion. *Inclusion and Democracy*. New York: Oxford University Press, 2000.
Zinn, Howard. *A People's History of the United States*. New York: Harper and Row, 1980.

INDEX

African Americans
  civil rights and, 37, 48
  and labor unions, 79, 84
  and New Deal coalition, 36, 48, 67, 68, 87
  in 1936 campaign, 18, 80–86, 113, 116, 117
Agricultural Administration Act, 15, 34, 74, 102
America First, 45
American Indians, 36
American Liberty League, 9, 21
  and 1936 election, 14–15, 45, 46
  opposition to FDR, 32, 103–4
  as problem for the Republican Party, 17, 103, 105, 107
Antilynching Bill, 37, 48
anti-Semitism, U.S., 47, 48

Bank of the United States, 5
Black Cabinet, 82
Black Tuesday, 5
Borah, William, 104
Brian Trust, 34–35
Brown decision, 86
Bund, German American, 49
Bush, George H. W., 119

Catholics, American, 18, 48, 67, 111. *See also* New Deal coalition
candidate-centered campaigns, 4, 21, 43–44, 46, 62–64, 113, 119
civil rights, 37, 48
Civilian Conservation Corps, 7, 85
Clark, Bennett Champ, 55. *See also* Committee of One
class, social
  and African Americans, 84–85
  as a campaign issue, 10, 12, 17, 93, 98, 102, 109, 111
  and organized labor, 72–73, 78
clergy letters, 33–37
Clinton, Bill, 119

Committee of One, 16, 19, 21, 46–47, 64, 97
  role in 1936 campaign, 43, 54–65
Communist Party, American, 9, 47, 49, 82
Congress, U.S., 14
  Roosevelt's attempted purge of, 8, 62, 78
Constitution, U.S., 8, 15
Coughlin, Father Charles E., 9–10, 11, 17, 48
  as opponent of FDR, 11, 31, 107–8, 110
  See also Union Party
court-packing, 8 n. 28, 14, 78, 102
Cummings, Homer, 104
Cutting, Bronson, 15

democratic deliberation, 2, 3, 5, 13, 25, 47, 65, 91. *See also* polls, public opinion
Democratic Party, 13
  "Colored" Division, 82–83
  Labor Division, 77–80
  National Committee, 16, 20, 120
  National Convention (1936), 16, 30 91–92
  Women's Division, 16, 19, 67, 69–77, 101
  See also Dewson, Mary W.
Depression, Great, 5, 13, 54
  as a crisis of political authority, 89–90, 122
  disproportionate effects of, 69, 77, 78, 81–82
  importance as 1936 campaign issue, 36, 48
Dewson, Mary W., 21, 67, 116, 120, 121
  biography and political involvement of, 69–71
  campaign materials of, 71–77, 83, 84
  as campaign surrogate, 99, 104
  and Democratic Party, 24, 70, 74, 75
  use of technology, 75–76
  Western Tour, 40
  See also Women's Division of the Democratic National Committee

Early, Stephen, 30
election (1934), 12–13

election (1936)
    campaign chronology, 14–20
    campaign communication, 55–60
    as a deliberative event, 2, 4–5, 13–14, 94–95
    finances and, 19
    as historic, 1–2
    voter mobilization, 56–57, 66–88
Equal Rights Amendment, 69

Farley, James, 42
    correspondence of, 29, 38, 41
    and conduct of 1936 campaign, 16, 19, 28–32, 114
    as Democratic Party Chair, 24, 28, 55–56
    patronage, 28, 30
    as political aide, 28, 43
    relationship with FDR, 31, 32, 33
Federal Emergency Relief Administration, 7
Fish, Hamilton, 104

Gallup, George, 26–27, 38
Germany, 5
Good Neighbor League, 16, 19, 20–21, 64, 97
    and democratic deliberation, 51–52
    and race, 84, 85
    role in 1936 campaign, 43, 46–47, 50–54, 101

Hastings, Daniel, 15
Hearst, William Randolph, 10
High, Stanley, 97
Hitler, Adolf, 5
Hoover, Herbert, 10, 80, 103, 110
Hundred Days, 6–7
Hurja, Emil
    and history of polling, 20, 38
    and 1936 election, 24, 38–41, 114

Ickes, Harold, 104, 107
interest groups, 66, 79
    as constituent parts of electorate, 4, 14, 87
    and democracy, 67, 87–88, 113, 116–17

Jackson, Andrew, 7, 89, 94
Japan, 5
Jews, American, 18, 48, 52, 67, 111. *See also* anti-Semitism, U.S.; New Deal coalition
Johnson, Hiram, 104

Krock, Arthur, 9, 13, 80 n. 73
Ku Klux Klan, 15, 49

labor, organized, 68, 113, 116, 117
    as members of New Deal Coalition, 12, 79
    and 1936 election, 67, 77–80
    and racial tensions, 79
    and Social Security, 79
    See also Lewis, John L.
Landon, Alf, 21, 31
    as campaigner, 16, 19, 104–7
    as compromise candidate, 15, 104
    Democrat's attack on 32, 61
    depiction of FDR, 105–6
    as moderate voice, 17, 104, 108
    Roosevelt's depiction of, 90
    standing in public opinion polls, 18
    supporters of, 103–4
Lazelle, Louise, 53
Lemke, William, 18
Lend-Lease, 45
Lewis, John L., 78, 121
Lincoln, Abraham, 89
Lippmann, Walter, 15
Long, Huey, 10, 16, 31–32

Maine, 1, 32
mass media, 1, 4, 16, 121
McGovern-Fraser, 29
Mexico, 48
Morgan, J. P., 61
Morgenthau, Henry, 51

NAACP, 83
National Industrial Recovery Act, 6–7, 9, 68, 79
    invalidation by Supreme Court, 13
    opposition to, 34
    as a programmatic failure, 6–7
    See also Black Tuesday
New Deal
    coalition, 12, 18, 36 n. 73, 44–49, 78, 81, 113
    as issue in 1936 campaign, 32, 35, 60
    philosophy of, 52, 54, 67, 97
    programs, 6, 10, 13, 31, 41
    public opinion and, 10, 33
    and race, 84, 85
    reforms, 8, 69
    supporters of, 9, 15
    and women, 74–77
Norris, George W., 15
Nye, Gerald, 15

Obama, Barack, 119–20, 121
organizational politics, 3, 29, 119 n. 8, 83
    as extra-partisan, 43–47, 56–57, 86–87

parties, political, 7, 45–47, 50, 55, 115–16
Pepper, George Wharton, 108–9
Perkins, Frances, 63, 69, 76, 78
Pinchot, Gifford, 104
polls, public opinion
  as measure of public opinion, 1, 3, 62
  in 1936 election, 38–42, 62
  and public deliberation, 20, 23, 24–25, 37, 114–15
Powell, Adam Clayton, 85
Progressives
  Party, 11, 51
  philosophy and policies, 26, 29, 69, 120
Prohibition (and Repeal), 34
Protestants, 18
public opinion, 23, 26–27, 37, 39–42, 89, 122

Raskob, John Jacob, 103. *See also* American Liberty League
Reagan, Ronald, 119
Republican Party, 14, 21, 104–7, 117–18
  Progressive wing, 15
  Republican convention (1936), 15–16
  general election campaign, 104–7
rhetorical presidency, 4, 7 n. 26, 26, 89
Romney, Mitt, 121
Roosevelt, Eleanor, 24, 69, 80
Roosevelt, Franklin D.
  accusations of dictatorial power, 8–9, 101, 109
  administrative capacity, 7, 43–47
  and business, 18, 59, 97, 99, 102
  as campaign issue, 32, 61
  and citizenship, 59–60, 68, 73–74, 96, 98–99, 111, 112–13
  and civil rights, 37, 48, 80–81, 82–83
  and Congress, 7–8, 40–41, 56
  correspondence, 24
  critics of, 8–12, 89, 102–10
  and democratic deliberation, 2–3, 4, 90
  and the Democratic Party, 7, 13, 44–48, 50, 62–65, 68, 75
  depiction of opposition, 93–94, 95, 100–101
  executive power and, 7, 8–9, 29, 90–93, 94, 100
  fireside chats, 6
  and interest groups, 66–68
  and labor, 18, 78
  leadership, 5, 7, 27, 37, 91
  legacy of, 27, 63, 64–65, 114, 115, 117, 118–22
  legislative agenda, 7, 72, 92
  and mass media, 92, 99

  1932 election, 5, 19, 89–102, 112
  political philosophy, 12–13, 27, 33, 49, 54, 62, 98, 113
  popularity, 12, 24, 39
  as presidential candidate in 1936, 1, 18, 31
  political rhetoric of, 4, 17, 41, 55, 90, 95–102
  and public opinion, 24, 27, 101, 110, 114–15
  and religious groups, 18, 95–96, 111, 114
  and urban vote, 18, 111
  See also New Deal; clergy letters; court-packing; Congress, U.S.,
Roosevelt, Theodore, 26, 83, 89

Second New Deal, 8, 13
Scopes trial, 26
Scottsboro Boys, 81–82
Share the Wealth program, 31–32
Shouse, Jouett, 9
Silver, Nate, 38, 114
Socialists, American, 18
Social Security, 120
  as campaign issue, 17–18, 36, 53, 75–76, 79–80, 99, 106–7
Smith, Al, 9, 15, 53, 110
Smith, Gerald K., 10, 16, 107
Smoot-Hawley Act, 5
Stayton, William H., 103. *See also* American Liberty League
Stetzle, Charles, 50. *See also* Good Neighbor League
Supreme Court, U.S., 8, 53, 78, 82, 119. *See also* court-packing

Tammany Hall, 28
Thomas, Norman, 18
Townsend, Dr. Francis, 11
  Townsendites, 31, 47
  Townsend Plan, 36
  See also Union Party

Union Party, 10, 107
USSR, 35, 48

Vermont, 1, 32
voter mobilization, 3, 4, 19, 67–88. *See also* organizational politics

Wagner Labor Relations Act, 68, 78, 79
Wallace, Henry, 104, 107
White Committee, 45
Wilson, Woodrow, 26, 89

Winant, John C., 53
Women's Division of the Democratic National Committee, 16, 19, 67, 69–77, 84, 101. *See also* Dewson, Mary W.
Works Progress Administration, 36, 40, 74
World War I, 5
World War II, 45
Wright, Bishop R. R., 85

RHETORIC AND DEMOCRATIC DELIBERATION

Other books in the series:

Karen Tracy, *Challenges of Ordinary Democracy: A Case Study in Deliberation and Dissent* / VOLUME 1

Samuel McCormick, *Letters to Power: Public Advocacy Without Public Intellectuals* / VOLUME 2

Christian Kock and Lisa S. Villadsen, eds., *Rhetorical Citizenship and Public Deliberation* / VOLUME 3

Jay P. Childers, *The Evolving Citizen: American Youth and the Changing Norms of Democratic Engagement* / VOLUME 4

Dave Tell, *Confessional Crises: Confession and Cultural Politics in Twentieth-Century America* / VOLUME 5

David Boromisza-Habashi, *Speaking Hatefully: Culture, Public Communication, and Political Action in Hungary* / VOLUME 6

Arabella Lyon, *Deliberative Acts: Democracy, Rhetoric, and Rights* / VOLUME 7

Lyn Carson, John Gastil, Janette Hartz-Karp, and Ron Lubensky, eds., *The Australian Citizens' Parliament and the Future of Deliberative Democracy* / VOLUME 8

Christa Olson, *Constitutive Visions: Indigeneity and Commonplaces of National Identity in Republican Ecuador* / VOLUME 9

Damien Smith Pfister, *Networked Media, Networked Rhetorics: Attention and Deliberation in the Early Blogosphere* / VOLUME 10

Katherine Elizabeth Mack, *From Apartheid to Democracy: Deliberating Truth and Reconciliation in South Africa* / VOLUME 11

Typeset by
BOOKCOMP, INC.

Printed and bound by
SHERIDAN BOOKS

Composed in
MINION PRO AND SCALA

Printed on
NATURES NATURAL

Bound in
ARRESTOX

www.ingramcontent.com/pod-product-compliance
Lightning Source LLC
Chambersburg PA
CBHW021408290426
44108CB00010B/439